The
AUSTRALIAN
MISCELLANY

The
AUSTRALIAN
MISCELLANY

Containing a Great Many
Astonishing Facts

DAVID MORGAN

BANTAM
SYDNEY • AUCKLAND • TORONTO • NEW YORK • LONDON

THE AUSTRALIAN MISCELLANY
A BANTAM BOOK

First published in Australia and New Zealand in 2005
by Bantam

National Library of Australia
Cataloguing-in-Publication Entry

Morgan, David (David James), 1961- .
  Australian miscellany.

  ISBN 1 86325 537 0.

  1. Curiosities and wonders - Australia. 2. Australia -
  Miscellanea. I. Title.

994

Transworld Publishers,
a division of Random House Australia Pty Ltd
20 Alfred Street, Milsons Point, NSW 2061
http://www.randomhouse.com.au

Random House New Zealand Limited
18 Poland Road, Glenfield, Auckland

Transworld Publishers,
a division of The Random House Group Ltd
61–63 Uxbridge Road, Ealing, London W5 5SA

Random House Inc
1745 Broadway, New York, New York 10036

Cover and text designed by Darian Causby/Highway 51 Design Works
Cover illustration by Michael Perkins
Typeset by Midland Typesetters, Australia
Printed and bound by Griffin Press, Netley, South Australia

10 9 8 7 6 5 4 3 2 1

For the five most important women in my life:
My wife, Katie
My daughter, Rosemary Jean
My sister, Ann-Maree
My mother, Noela (1925–2003)
My aunt, Jean Culverwell (1924–2001)

INTRODUCTION

This book does not claim to be comprehensive, though it may help you with pub trivia nights. It is a grab bag of Australiana past, present, and occasionally might-have-been, haphazardly but heroically thrown together. It is as accurate as I can make it at time of writing, but advise you not to rely on it for anything important. I just hope you enjoy it.

I could be serious and remind you of Kenneth Clark's belief that we must try to learn from history because 'History is ourselves', or Simon Schama's view that 'To have a future at all presupposes keeping faith with the past'. But for so many people, learning about Australia and its history is rather like eating spinach: '*I know you don't like it, dear, but it's good for you*'. If you find this book to be more like macadamia nuts – tasty and all-Australian, though rather easier to crack – then I'll consider it a success.

AN EXTREMELY SHORT HISTORY OF AUSTRALIA

Gondwanaland – Megafauna – Humans arrive – Hartog –
Macassans visit – Tasman – Cook – First Fleet – Convicts –
Bennelong – Flinders – Bligh – Rum – Wool – Macquarie –
Wentworth – Black resistance – Batman – Chisholm – Myall Creek
massacre – Gold! – Eureka – Responsible government – Football –
Rabbits – 'Dig' – Overland Telegraph – Truganini – Ned Kelly –
Sudan – BHP – Ashes – Depression – ALP – Flack – Melba –
McKillop – Federation – White Australia – Women vote –
Arbitration – Gallipoli – France – Conscription – Monash –
Vegemite – Coniston massacre – 'Mo' – Depression – Lang – Phar
Lap – Bradman – Tobruk – Curtin – Singapore – Darwin – Kokoda
– Milne Bay – Florey – Changi – Holden – Snowy – Migrants –
Menzies – ANZUS – TV – Olympics – Dawn – Colombo Plan –
Murdoch – *Oz* – Vietnam – Gurindji strike – Women's lib – Films –
Hogan – 'It's Time' – Recession – Dismissal – Boat people – No gold
medals! – Hawke – America's Cup – Gulf War – Recession – Mabo
– APEC – Howard – Hanson – Port Arthur – Republic – East Timor
– Cathy and Thorpedo – Afghanistan – Bali – Iraq.

WHAT THEY THOUGHT OF AUSTRALIA

'That intolerable continent.'
Lord Kenneth Clark

'I like Australia and I love your oysters.'
Noël Coward

'Nothing ever happens in Woy Woy.'
Spike Milligan

'This is the most democratic country I have *ever* been in.
And the more I see of democracy the more I dislike it.'
D. H. Lawrence

THE AUSTRALIAN ACCENT

What puzzles me exceedingly to account for, a very large proportion of both male and female native snuffle dreadfully; just the same nasal twang the Americans have. In some cases, English parents have come out here with English-born children; these all speak clearly and well and continue to do so, whilst those born after the parents arrive in the colony have the detestable snuffle. This is an enigma which passes my sagacity to solve.

Mrs Charles Meredith,
Notes and Sketches of New South Wales, 1844

SOME NOTED POLISH–AUSTRALIANS

Anna Broinowski...*filmmaker*
Richard Broinowski ....*diplomat*
Paul 'The Count' Grabowsky ....*composer*
Michael Klim ....*swimmer*
Karl Kruszelnicki ....*scientist*
Peter Skrzynecki ....*poet*
'Count' Paul Strzelecki ....*explorer*
Zygmunt 'Ziggy' Switkowski ....CEO of Telstra 1999–2005
Magda Szubanski ....*actor*
Tom Zubrycki...*film director*
Jerzy Zubrzycki....................*'father of multiculturalism in Australia'*

Note: Magda Szubanski's character in the television comedy *Kath and Kim* was called 'Sharon Strzlecki'.

TO KEEP SNAKES AWAY

Snakes may be permanently driven from a place by planting geraniums freely about the house and grounds.

The Australian Woman's Magazine and Domestic Journal, 1883

BORDER TOWNS

Town	State	Border
Goondiwindi	Qld	NSW
Texas	Qld	NSW
Hungerford	Qld	NSW
Barringun	NSW	Qld
Coolangatta	Qld	NSW (Tweed Heads)*
Queanbeyan	NSW	ACT
Wallangarra	Qld	NSW
Delegate River	Vic	NSW
Tintaldra	Vic	NSW
Jingellic	NSW	Vic
Howlong	NSW	Vic
Corowa	NSW	Vic (Wahgunya)*
Barham	NSW	Vic (Koondrook)*
Mulwala	NSW	Vic (Yarrawonga)*
Albury	NSW	Vic (Wodonga)*
Tocumwal	NSW	Vic
Barmah	Vic	NSW
Echuca	Vic	NSW (Moama)*
Swan Hill	Vic	NSW
Piangil	Vic	NSW
Robinvale	Vic	NSW
Wentworth	NSW	Vic
Donovans Landing	SA	Vic
Cockburn	SA	NSW
Border Village	SA	WA

*Different names on either side of the border
Note: Bordertown, SA, is actually 18 kilometres west of the SA/Victoria border, so is not a border town.

3

DEGREES OF SEPARATION

1. Queen Elizabeth II and Ned Kelly
Queen Elizabeth II
often met her grandfather
King George V
who in 1919 knighted the Australian General
Sir John Monash
who as a schoolboy on holiday from Melbourne
was in Jerilderie, NSW, in 1878 when the bushranger
Ned Kelly
and his gang rode into town.

2. Paul Keating and Adolf Hitler
Paul Keating
was a protégé of former NSW Premier
Jack Lang
who in Sydney in 1920 as Treasurer met the visiting
Duke of Windsor (then Prince of Wales, later King Edward VIII)
who in 1938 on a visit to Germany after
his abdication met the Führer
Adolf Hitler

3. Molly Meldrum and Nikita Khrushchev
Ian 'Molly' Meldrum
who on *Countdown* hosted Edna Everage, the alter ego of
Barry Humphries
who frequently met the historian
Manning Clark
who frequently met the historian, politician and Governor-General
Paul Hasluck
who on a visit to Moscow in 1965 met the Soviet Premier
Aleksei Kosygin
who had recently been part of the overthrow of
Soviet Communist Party Secretary
Nikita Khrushchev

4. Dick Smith and Albert Einstein
Dick Smith
the aviator, publisher and businessman is the grandson
of the noted Sydney photographer
Harold Cazneaux
who in 1935 photographed the visiting violin virtuoso
Yehudi Menuhin
who was playing in Berlin in 1929 when
Albert Einstein
heard him and reportedly met him backstage, telling him
'Now I know there is a God in heaven.'

ULTIMO, NOT INSTANT

The inner Sydney suburb of Ultimo is named after the Ultimo
Estate, the home of Surgeon John Harris (1754–1838), an officer of
the New South Wales Corps. The unusual name derived from an
incident during Harris's time as a magistrate. He backed Governor
Philip Gidley King in conflicts with senior officers of the Corps, and
as a result of his handling of a court-martial was himself court-
martialled in 1803. The charge incorrectly stated that his offence
had taken place on 'the 19th ultimo' (last month) rather than 'the
19th instant' (this month). Because of this error, King was able have
the 'guilty' verdict set aside. The Harris family remained prominent
in Sydney life, with two of Surgeon John's great-nephews becoming
Lord Mayors of Sydney.

Source: City of Sydney History Program

ADJECTIVES POPULARISED AS NOUNS BY PMs

Paul Keating (on Dr Mahathir in 1993): *recalcitrant*
John Howard: *tragic (as in 'cricket tragic')*

THE FACES ON OUR BANKNOTES

The coronation of Queen Elizabeth II in 1953 saw the issue of a new series of Australian banknotes, the first to feature portraits of people who played a major role in Australian history:

10s **Matthew Flinders** (1774–1814), circumnavigated Australia and promoted the name 'Australia', with Parliament House, Canberra, on the reverse.

£1 **Queen Elizabeth II** (1926–) with explorers Charles Sturt (1795–1869) and Hamilton Hume (1797–1872) on the reverse.

£5 **John Franklin** (1796–1847), explorer and Lieutenant-Governor of Tasmania, with agriculture and indigenous themes on the reverse.

£10 **Arthur Phillip** (1738–1814), first Governor of NSW, with industry and science themes on the reverse.

The introduction of decimal currency in 1966 led to a new series. With some exceptions, the notes featured a portrait on each side:

$1 **Queen Elizabeth II** with Aboriginal art on the reverse. (Replaced by coin, 1984.)

$2 **John Macarthur** (1767–1834), wool industry pioneer, and **William Farrer** (1845–1906), developer of rust-resistant wheat. (Replaced by coin, 1988.)

$5 **Sir Joseph Banks** (1743–1820), botanist on Cook's first voyage (and thereafter an 'expert' on Australia) and President of the Royal Society, and **Caroline Chisholm** (1808–1877), promoter of settlement by women.

$10 **Francis Greenway** (1777–1837), emancipist architect, and **Henry Lawson** (1867–1922), poet and short-story writer.

$20 **Sir Charles Kingsford-Smith** (1897–1935), aviator, and **Lawrence Hargrave** (1850–1915), aeronautical inventor.

$50 (first issued 1973) **Howard Florey** (1898–1968), developer of penicillin, and **Ian Clunies-Ross** (1899–1959), chairman of CSIRO 1949–1959.

$100 (first issued 1984) **Douglas Mawson** (1882–1959), Antarctic explorer, and **John Tebbutt** (1834–1916), astronomer.

In 1988, a polymer substrate $10 note was issued to commemorate the Bicentenary of British settlement. Then from 1994 paper notes were gradually phased out, to be replaced with the new forgery-proof material, and some familiar faces disappeared:

$5   **Queen Elizabeth II** with an aerial view of Parliament House, Canberra, on the reverse.
$5   (first issued 2001) **Henry Parkes** (1815–1896), the 'Father of Federation', and **Catherine Helen Spence** (1825–1910), novelist and electoral reformer.
$10   **A. B. 'Banjo' Paterson** (1864–1941) and **Dame Mary Gilmore** (1865–1962), both poets and journalists.
$20   **Mary Reibey** (1777–1855), emancipist businesswoman, and **The Rev. John Flynn** (1880–1951) founder of Royal Flying Doctor Service.
$50   **David Unaipon** (1872–1967), writer and inventor, and **Edith Cowan** (1861–1932), first female parliamentarian.
$100   **Dame Nellie Melba** (1861–1931), opera singer, and **Sir John Monash** (1865–1931), soldier and engineer.

ANIMAL PASSIONS OF THE AUSTRALIAN MALE

'To the highest type of man the highest consummation of love is the indulgence of an animal passion. To a woman, physical manifestations . . . deteriorate rather than enhance the beauty and spirituality of love. The gulf between them is bridged by women's self-sacrifice and man's self-indulgence – but for how long? Man's selfish animalism is driving women in the opposite direction and these unsympathetic relations have more to do with conjugal misery than anything else.'

Rose Scott (1847–1925)
pioneer Australian feminist.

TWO TYPES OF AUSSIE PLACE NAME

RESOUNDING!	Banal
Archipelago of the Recherche	Ayers Rock
Cape Tribulation	Big Desert
Charters Towers	Central Station, Sydney
Great Barrier Reef	Main Beach, Qld
Joseph Bonaparte Gulf	Naval Base, WA
Kakadu	North, Middle and South Heads, Sydney
Koo Wee Rup	Northern Territory
Mt Kosciuszko	Snowy Mountains
Nullarbor Plain	South Australia
Tasmania	Sydney Cricket Ground
The Gabba	Sydney Entertainment Centre
The Twelve Apostles	Sydney Exhibition Centre
Tibooburra	Sydney Football Stadium
Uluru	Sydney Harbour Bridge
Walls of Jerusalem	Sydney Opera House
Woolloomooloo	Western Australia

COMMONLY MISPRONOUNCED OR MISSPELT

Albany, WA	*'Awl-bany'*
Australia	*'Aw-stralya'* (by the Queen)
Cairns, Qld	*'Cans'*
Castlemaine, Vic	*'Cah-sul-main'* (by non-Victorians)
Forster, NSW	*'Foster'*
Jervis Bay, NSW/ACT	*'Jarvis Bay'*
Melbourne, Vic	*Mel-borne'* (by Americans)
Mosman, NSW	*'Mozman'* (by arrivistes)
Newcastle, NSW	*'New-cassle'* (by Victorians)
Surfers Paradise, Qld	*'Surface Paradise'*

POLLIES SQUAWK

Dame Enid Lyons, first woman member, House of Representatives (1943–1951)
In her maiden speech, 1943 on being called a new broom: 'I hold firm views on brooms and sweeping.'

Arthur Calwell, Immigration Minister 1946–1949
On non-white immigration, 1972: 'No red-blooded Australian wants to see a chocolate-coloured Australia in the 1980s.'

Robert Menzies, Prime Minister 1949–1966
When asked, 'Wotcha gunna do about 'ousing?' Menzies replied: 'Put an "H" in front of it.'

Sir Henry Bolte, Premier of Victoria 1955–1972
On striking rail workers: 'They can march up and down until they're bloody well footsore.'

Sir Robert Askin, Premier of NSW 1965–1974
On demonstrators against visiting US President Lyndon Johnson: 'Run over the bastards.'

Gough Whitlam, Prime Minister 1972–1975
On being sacked, 1975: 'Well may we say "God save the Queen" – because nothing will save the Governor-General. The proclamation you have just heard read by the Governor-General's official secretary was countersigned "Malcolm Fraser" – who will undoubtedly go down in history, from Remembrance Day 1975, as "Kerr's cur".'

Paul Keating, Prime Minister 1991–1996
On Opposition Leader John Hewson: 'Like being flogged with a warm lettuce.'

ORIGINS OF THE NAMES OF THE MEMBERS
OF 'THIS IS SERIOUS MUM' (TISM)

I have taken it upon myself to decipher the names of these mysterious musicians for your benefit, dear reader:

Ron Hitler-Barassi
From Adolf Hitler (1889–1945), German Führer 1933–1945 and Ron Barassi (1936–), former Australian Rules football player, coach and motivational speaker.

Humphrey B. Flaubert
From Gustave Flaubert (1821–1880), French novelist (*Madame Bovary*) and Humphrey B. Bear (1965–), children's television character.

Leak Van Vlalen
Unclear, but all suggestions welcome.

Tokin Blackman
A pun on 'token black man' (one employed to give an impression of racial equality where it does not exist) and 'toking' (smoking marijuana).

Jock Cheese
Possibly a variation on John Cleese (1939–), British comedian (*Fawlty Towers*).

Jon St. Peenis
From John St Peeters, Australian singer–songwriter and musician, who frequently appeared on *The Mike Walsh Show* in the 1970s and '80s. Walsh once described St Peeters as 'a very original and a very stylish performer'.

Eugene De La Hot Croix-Bun
From Eugene Delacroix (1798–1863), French Romantic painter (*Liberty Leading the People*) and the Easter delicacy.

Les Miserables
From the novel by Victor Hugo (1802–1885), although 'Les' is probably pronounced as though his first name is 'Leslie'.

According to their 1988 album, *Great Truckin' Songs of the Renaissance*, other characters associated with TISM include: 'The Most Beautiful Economist in the World', '"Action" Greggers', 'Richard "The Crusher" Vomit' and 'The Slave to the Economist'. Several websites devoted to TISM, which may or may not have direct TISM involvement, have also included an abusive screed about them written by 'Rod Agonistes', whose name comes from John Milton's *Samson Agonistes*, possibly via T. S. Eliot's *Sweeney Agonistes*. All these references, combined with the fact that they only tour during school holidays (wearing balaclavas to mask their identities), have led to speculation that TISM are actually school teachers.

ORIGIN OF THE AUSTRALIAN FEATURE FILM RENAISSANCE OF THE 1970s

I wrote a report to [Prime Minister John] Gorton: 'It's time to see our own landscapes, hear our own voices and dream our own dreams.' The very first film to be financed by the film bank was a very sensitive film, a very beautiful film. It was called The Adventures of Barry McKenzie.

Phillip Adams
ABC–TV interview

STATE BIRD EMBLEMS

ACT ....*Gang-gang cockatoo*	SA......*Piping shrike (unofficial)*
NSW ....*Kookaburra*	Tasmania ....—
NT ....*Wedge-tailed eagle*	Victoria ...*Helmeted honeyeater*
Queensland....................*Brolga*	WA ....*Black swan*

THE BOMBING OF DARWIN, 19 FEBRUARY 1942:
SOME STATISTICS

Raids: 2
Attacking aircraft: 54 land-based, 188 carrier-based
Initial official death toll: 17
Actual death toll: 243 (including 31 civilians)
Wounded: 300–400
Servicemen still missing three days after 'Adelaide River Stakes': 278
Ships sunk: 8
Timeline (from an official report):

0959	Japanese aircraft over area
1005	McMillans engaging
1006	Fannie Bay engaging
	Berrimah engaging with LMG
1029	Machine gunning Berrimah
1030	Machine gunning Elliott Point and Berrimah
1031	Machine gunning McMillans
1048	Sound all clear
1210	Planes approaching McMillans
1213	Alarm to RAAF
	Fannie Bay engaging
1215	Planes bombing Ironstone
1216	Direct hits by bombs on RAAF
1235	Vestey's on fire – RAAF on fire
1304	All clear

Note: Subsequent raids on Darwin until December 1943 totalled 63

BE WARY OF THE CASSOWARY

The cassowary is a large flightless bird found in the rainforests of north Queensland and New Guinea. Fully grown, the cassowary weighs about 60 kilograms. It has powerful legs and if provoked may kick in self-defence: its inner toe has a very large, sharp claw, which makes it capable of killing humans.

SOME FIRSTS FOR AUSTRALIAN WOMEN

First newspaper editor ....Elizabeth MacFarrell, 1846
(Perth *Gazette*)

First published novelist........................Catherine Helen Spence, 1854
(*Clara Morison*)

First Australian-born novelist..........Caroline Louisa Atkinson, 1857
(*Gertrude the Emigrant*)

First accepted into university.............University of Melbourne, 1880

First graduate university ....Bella Guerin, 1883
(BA, Uni. of Melbourne)

First to practise medicine...Constance Stone,
Melbourne, 1890

First obtained the vote................................. the women of SA, 1894

First law graduate...Ada Emily Evans, 1902
(Uni. of Sydney)

First Olympic gold medal
 (and first for Australia) ....Fanny Durack, 1912
(100 m freestyle)

First elected to parliament ....Edith Cowan, 1921
(Seat of West Perth, State parliament)

First to obtain pilot's licence ....Millicent Bryant, 1927

First Mayor...Lillian Fowler, 1938
(Newtown, NSW)

First QC ....Dame Roma Mitchell, 1962

First Supreme Court Judge.....................Dame Roma Mitchell, 1965

First Women's Adviser to the
 Prime Minister (also a world first) .... Elizabeth Reid, 1973

First Lord Mayor ....Joy Cummings, 1974
(Newcastle, NSW)

First leader of a parliamentary ....Janine Haines, 1986
 political party   (Australian Democrats)

First jockey in Melbourne Cup ....Maree Lyndon, 1987

First Premier ....Carmen Lawrence, 1990 (WA)

First president of the ACTU...............................Jennie George, 1995

First to lead a police force ....Christine Nixon, 2001

BIG . . .

Apple ....Stanthorpe, Qld
Donnybrook, WA
Avocado.........Byron Bay, NSW
Axe ....Kew, NSW
Ayers Rock* ....Karuah, NSW
Banana ....Coffs Harbour,
NSW
Barramundi ....Daintree, Qld
Normanton, Qld
Beer Can and
Burger............Claremont, WA
Bottle......Mangrove Mountain,
NSW
Bull................Wauchope, NSW
Rockhampton, Qld
Cane Toad** ....Gordonvale,
Qld
Captain Cook ....Cairns, Qld
Cassowary........Mission Beach,
Qld
Cheese....................Bega, NSW
Cherries ....Young, NSW
Cigar ....Churchill, Vic
Cigarette ....Myrtleford, Vic
Cow ....Nambour, Qld
Crocodile ....Wyndham, WA
Normanton, Qld
Dice ....Broken Hill, NSW
Fruit Bowl ....Bilpin, NSW
Galah ....Kimba, SA
Guitar (Golden) ......Tamworth,
NSW
Guitar (Playable)...Narrandera,
NSW
Gumboot..................Tully, Qld

Koala ....Dadswell Bridge, Vic
Koalas ....Coffs Harbour,
NSW
Lobster ....Kingston, SA
Macadamia ....Nambour, Qld
Mallee Root............Ouyen, Vic
Mandarin ....Mundubbera, Qld
Marlin ....Cairns, Queensland
Matchsticks*** ....Sydney,
NSW
Merino ....Goulburn, NSW
Milkshake...........Kyabram, Vic
Miner's Lamp....Lithgow, NSW
Mosquito ....Hexham, NSW
Murray Cod ......Swan Hill, Vic
Ned Kelly ....Glenrowan, Vic
Orange ....Harvey, WA
Tenterfield, NSW
Gayndah, Qld
Berri, SA
Oyster ....Taree, NSW
Peanut...........North Tolga, Qld
Penguin.................Penguin, Vic
Pineapple...........Nambour, Qld
Potato............Robertson, NSW
Prawn ....Ballina, NSW
Ram ....Wagin, WA
Rock.....Barrington Tops, NSW
Rocking Horse ......Gumeracha,
SA
Rolling Pin ....Wodonga, Vic
Slide Rule ....School of
Mathematics and Physics,
University of Tasmania,
Hobart, Tas

Submarine**** ....Holbrook, NSW
Sundial ....Singleton, NSW
Trout ....Adaminaby, NSW
Winch ....Coober Pedy, SA

Windmill ....Coffs Harbour, NSW
Wool Bales ....Hamilton, Vic
Worm ....Bass, Vic

* The 'Big Ayers Rock' at the now-closed Leyland Brothers World was actually smaller than life size.
** The 'Big Cane Toad' was proposed in the 1980s but never built.
*** Standing on the slope at the rear of the Art Gallery of NSW, the 'Big Matchsticks' – one burnt out, one unused – are the work of Brett Whiteley (see Archibald Prize).
**** The 'Big Submarine' is life size: it is the actual above-waterline structure of HMAS *Otway*.

THE TOP 10 FERAL SPECIES

Species	Damage
1. Carp	Pushing native fish to the edge of extinction, increasing turbidity, erosion and nutrients in the Murray–Darling, passing along viruses.
2. Rabbit	Annual cost to pastures: $600 million.
3. Blackberry	Swamps native species, wipes out productive pastures, provides refuge to rabbits and foxes.
4. Pacific sea star	Eats scallops, abalone and other marine life.
5. Cane toad	Now threatening Kakadu National Park and NSW North Coast.
6. Mouse	Only exists in plague proportions in Australia.
7. European red fox	Eats native animals, and takes 10 to 30 per cent of all newborn sheep.
8. Red-legged earth mite	Eats pasture.
9. Sheep blowfly	Responsible for fly strike on sheep.
10. Serrated tussock	Made up of 90 per cent fibre and 4 per cent protein: animals eating it starve to death.

OUR PEST EXPORTS

While introduced species are a serious problem in Australia, the traffic has not all been one way:

Wallabies to New Zealand

This has nothing to do with rugby. First introduced in the 19th century for sport and for the value of their skins, by 1959 wallabies had been reported on more than 2,000,000 hectares, including pastoral land where they were accused of competing for food with sheep. They remain endemic on Kawau Island, 55 kilometres north-east of Auckland. However, it has been discovered that one sub-species now living on Kawau Island, the tammar wallaby, is descended from a subspecies which disappeared from the South Australian mainland in the early 1900s, and now only survives as an indigenous subspecies on Kangaroo Island. Since 2003, a project has been underway to repatriate the tammar wallaby to mainland South Australia and release it into the wild.

Eucalyptus to California

Blue gum eucalyptus was first cultivated in California as an ornamental plant. There was widespread commercial planting in the late 19th and early 20th centuries. California-grown eucalyptus proved to be unsuitable for building, so it was used mainly for fuel. It is most invasive in coastal areas subject to heavy summer fog (such as around San Francisco), and produces a chemical which leaches into the soil and inhibits the growth of indigenous plants. The trees and their bark litter are extremely flammable: California firefighters call them 'gasoline trees'. The eucalyptus had no natural enemies in California until 1984, when the eucalyptus longhorn borer (*Phoracantha semipunctata*) also found its way there from Australia.

Melaleuca to Florida

Introduced in 1907, the broad-leaved paperbark has successfully established itself across central and southern Florida and has been reported in Louisiana. It was planted as an ornamental plant and later utilised by developers to dry up wetlands. While it is considered good for erosion and flood control, and is used in a variety of commercial products including tea-tree oil, melaleuca establishes an exotic monoculture which blocks out light and provides a poor habitat for native species.

Macadamia to Hawaii and California

A rare example of a welcome Australian species. The macadamia was introduced into Hawaii in 1881 as an ornamental plant and for reforestation. The Hawaii Agricultural Experiment Station developed several promising strains in 1948, which led to the modern macadamia nut industry in Hawaii, later expanding to California. These days, macadamia nuts are a major export for Australia and are also grown commercially in countries such as Guatemala, Kenya and South Africa.

SOME OBSOLETE OR LITTLE USED
AUSTRALIAN SLANG

bonzer, bonza	good
clynah	girlfriend
come the raw prawn	seek an adavantage, try to impose on someone
the drum	reliable inside information
drongo	slow-witted person
lolly water	soft drink
motza	large amount of money
shickered	drunk
shoot through like a Bondi tram	to leave fast
skite	boast
stonkered	exhausted
stoush	fight
toey	restive

THE AUSTRALIAN JOCKEY CLUB DRESS CODE

In the Members' Enclosure at Royal Randwick, gentlemen are required to wear a suit, sports coat or blazer and tie – except during daylight saving, when coats need not be worn, provided braces are not showing. Ladies are expected to maintain a suitable standard in keeping with the dignity of the Members' Enclosure. Unacceptable attire includes:

Gentlemen
- Joggers, trackshoes or runners.
- Sandals, thongs, dilapidated footwear, scuffs or slippers.
- Footwear without socks.
- Jeans, jodhpurs, shorts or non-tailored slacks.
- Open neck shirts or shirts without a collar.
- Baseball caps or beanies.
- Pullovers or cardigans (without a jacket), rugby tops and football guernseys, even if wearing a tie.

Ladies
- Shorts, jeans or brief clothing.
- Pullovers, cardigans, parkas, duffle coats or waist length jackets.
- Jeans and shorts as outer wear.
- Running shoes including sandshoes, gymboots or thongs.

Source: The Australian Jockey Club

THE AUSTRALIAN CITIZENSHIP PLEDGE

From this time forward, under God*, I pledge my loyalty to Australia and its people, whose democratic beliefs I share, whose rights and liberties I respect, and whose laws I will uphold and obey.

*The pledge may be taken in the form of an affirmation, which does not include the words 'under God'.
Source: Department of Immigration and Multicultural and Indigenous Affairs

MERGERS, SPLITTINGS AND SACKINGS
OF SYDNEY CITY COUNCIL

1842   Council founded.

1853   NSW Government abolishes Council, appoints Commissioners.

1857   Council restored.

1909   Municipality of Camperdown added to City.

1928   NSW Government dismisses Council, appoints Commissioners.

1930   Council restored.

1948   Municipalities of Alexandria, Darlington, Erskineville (formerly Macdonaldtown), Newtown, Redfern, Waterloo, Paddington and Glebe transferred to City.

1966   NSW Government dismisses Council, appoints Commissioners.

1968   Glebe transferred to Municipality of Leichhardt, part of Paddington to Municipality of Woollahra, parts of Camperdown and Newtown to Municipality of Marrickville, the rest of the 1948 additions to the new Municipality of Northcott (later South Sydney).

1969   Council restored.

1982   South Sydney returns to City.

1987   NSW Government dismisses Council, appoints Commissioners.

1988   South Sydney removed from City, reducing it to 6.19 sq. km, smaller than its pre-1948 size.

1989   Council restored.

2003   Glebe returns to City from Leichhardt, Kings Cross returns from South Sydney.

2004   South Sydney returns to City.

Source: City of Sydney History Program

HOW TWO GIANTS OF
AUSTRALIAN HISTORY MET

According to Manning Clark, when he taught the History honours tutorial at Melbourne University in 1948 one of his students was so silent that Clark never learnt his name all through the first term. While the other students produced 'lively exchanges', this student never said anything, rarely smiled, seemed 'lost in the hubbub, all the clashes between the giants in the room'. At the end of the term one student submitted a brilliant essay, but the name meant nothing to Clark. When handing the essays back, he had to ask if a Mr Geoffrey Blainey was there. 'The silent one smiled, and reached out for the essay.'

OSCAR WILDE'S OPINION OF AUSTRALIA'S SHAPE

From his play, *Lady Windermere's Fan*:

HOPPER: How do you do, Lady Windermere? How do you do, Duchess? (*Bows to* LADY AGATHA.)

DUCHESS OF BERWICK: Dear Mr. Hopper, how nice of you to come so early. We all know how you are run after in London.

HOPPER: Capital place, London! They are not nearly so exclusive in London as they are in Sydney.

DUCHESS OF BERWICK: Ah! we know your value, Mr. Hopper. We wish there were more like you. It would make life so much easier. Do you know, Mr. Hopper, dear Agatha and I are so much interested in Australia. It must be so pretty with all the dear little kangaroos flying about. Agatha has found it on the map. What a curious shape it is! Just like a large packing case. However, it is a very young country, isn't it?

HOPPER: Wasn't it made at the same time as the others, Duchess?

DUCHESS OF BERWICK: How clever you are, Mr. Hopper. You have a cleverness quite your own.

THE AUSTRALIAN PAPERBACK

More than 30 years before Penguin Books released the paperbacks that revolutionised the worldwide booktrade, Australian Cecil Rowlandson (1865–1922) was selling paperback Australian novels for a shilling on railway bookstalls. The first 'Bookstall' paperback was *Sandy's Selection* by Steele Rudd, which appeared in 1904. By Rowlandson's death in 1922, his New South Wales Bookstall Company had published about 200 novels and sold nearly five million copies.

COMPARATIVE POPULATIONS OF HUMANS AND SHEEP

Census year	Humans	Sheep
1881	2 250 194	n.a.
1891	3 240 985	97 880 200
1901	3 773 801	70 613 100
1911	4 455 005	98 043 500
1921	5 435 734	81 611 400
1933	6 629 839	109 671 200
1947	7 579 358	95 466 800
1954	8 986 530	126 661 700
1961	10 508 186	152 384 000
1966	11 550 462	157 295 600
1971	12 755 638	177 532 500
1976	13 548 467	148 493 200
1981	14 926 800	134 308 100
1986	16 020 000	150 277 000
1991	16 852 258	163 237 600
1996	17 892 423	121 115 900
2001	18 972 350	110 927 700

Note: On 4 November 2003 the Australian Statistician announced that, using all the latest available information, it was estimated that Australia's population would reach 20,000,000 on 4 December, 2003. There was no prediction about sheep numbers.

BEER GLASS SIZES

New South Wales and ACT

Pint	568 ml	20 ounces
Schooner	425 ml	15 ounces
Middy	285 ml	10 ounces
Seven	200 ml	7 ounces
Pony	140 ml	5 ounces

Northern Territory

Schooner	425 ml	15 ounces
Handle	285 ml	10 ounces
Seven	200 ml	7 ounces

Queensland

Schooner	425 ml	15 ounces
Pot or Ten or Middy	285 ml	10 ounces
Beer or Seven	200 ml	7 ounces
Five (some pubs)	140 ml	5 ounces

South Australia

Pint ('reputed')	425 ml	15 ounces
Schooner	285 ml	10 ounces
Butcher	200 ml	7 ounces
Pony	140 ml	5 ounces

Tasmania

Ten or Pot/Handle	285 ml	10 ounces
Eight	225 ml	8 ounces
Six	170 ml	6 ounces
Small Beer	115 ml	4 ounces

Victoria

Pint	568 ml	20 ounces
Schooner	425 ml	15 ounces
Pot	285 ml	10 ounces
Glass	200 ml	7 ounces

Small Glass	170 ml	6 ounces
Pony	140 ml	5 ounces

Western Australia

Pot	575 ml	20 ounces
Schooner	425 ml	15 ounces
Middy	285 ml	10 ounces
Glass	200 ml	7 ounces
Bobbie	170 ml	6 ounces
Pony	140 ml	5 ounces
Shetland	115 ml	4 ounces

THE SIX O'CLOCK SWILL

Six o'clock closing for pubs was introduced in 1916 after a drunken riot among soldiers at the Liverpool, NSW, army camp. It was supposed to be abolished after the end of the First World War in 1918, but remained in place in all states until 1955, when it was abolished in NSW. Other states followed suit: the last was South Australia in 1967.

TO SAVE WATER DURING A PERTH DROUGHT

The late writer Geoffrey Dutton reported finding the following notice in a Perth hotel in 1979:

'Shower'
*Wet down, soap off, rinse off. Say about three minutes.
30 litres or less.*

'Bath'
May we suggest a shower. An average tub 70–90 litres.

'Washing Hands'
Place plug in basin NOT tap running. 3 litres.

JOHN McDOUALL STUART'S TRIUMPHAL
ENTRY INTO ADELAIDE, 1863

John McDouall Stuart succeeded where Burke and Wills failed in crossing Australia from south to north and back. But his remarkable achievement has been overshadowed by Burke and Wills' tragic failure.

However, according to a poster of the time, the people of Adelaide clearly thought otherwise when they welcomed Stuart to the city.

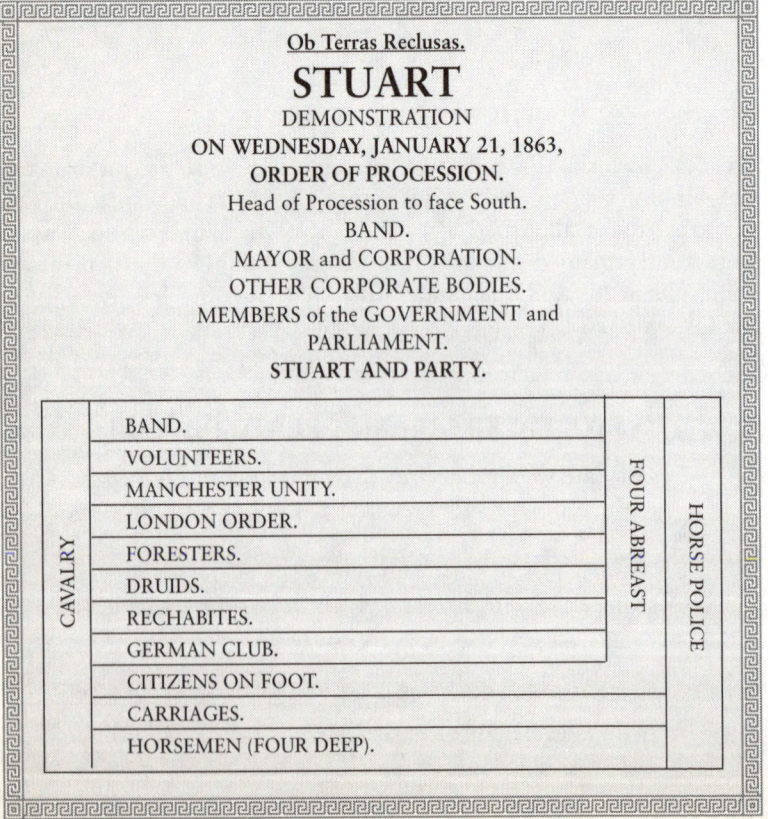

LIEUT.-Colonel FINNISS will be in Command of the Procession, assisted by Major MAYO.

ROUTE.

Procession to meet at North Adelaide, at the junction of O'Connell-street and Barton-terrace,

At HALF-PAST ONE p.m. Sharp,

So as to move off at TWO p.m. precisely, as follows:

Down O'Connell-street, Ward-street, Jeffcott-street, to pass the house of the late JAMES CHAMBERS, Esq., down Pennington-terrace, up King William-street to the Government Offices; when Mr. Stuart and party arrive opposite the Treasury

THE PROCESSION WILL HALT!

"THREE CHEERS!"

Mr. STUART will then present his dispatches to His Excellency Sir DOMINICK DALY. The MAYOR of ADELAIDE will read an ADDRESS to Mr. STUART, to be followed by the ADDRESSES of the various PUBLIC BODIES. The Procession will then disperse.

☞ *Gentlemen who have positions assigned them in the Procession, unless punctually in attendance, at the time of starting, will have to take their places in the rear.*

N.B. – Banquet at Aldridge's, at 7 p.m., His Excellency the Governor in the Chair.

W.A. CAWTHORNE, *Hon. Sec. Procession Committee.*

Note: 'Ob Terras Reclusas' was the motto of the Royal Geographical Society.

MATTHEW FLINDERS' CAT

On a window ledge behind the bronze statue of Matthew Flinders outside the State Library of NSW in Sydney there is a statue of his cat, Trim. He accompanied Flinders on the leaky HMS *Investigator* from 1801 to 1803, becoming the first cat to circumnavigate Australia. When Flinders was shipwrecked on HMS *Porpoise* on Wreck Reef off the Queensland coast while attempting to return to England in August 1803, Trim survived along with his master. They continued their journey on HMS *Cumberland*, but were unlucky enough to land in Mauritius, a French territory, after war between Britain and France had resumed. Flinders was detained there for 6½ years until in June 1810 the British, who were blockading the island, negotiated his release. During their captivity, Trim disappeared: stolen and eaten, Flinders believed, by hungry slaves. His tribute to Trim reads:

> [He was] one of the finest animals I ever saw . . . [his] robe was a clear jet black, with the exception of his four feet, which seemed to have been dipped in snow, and his under lip, which rivaled them in whiteness. He had also a white star on his breast.

The statue of Trim by John Cornwell was erected by 'The Friends of Trim' in 1995.

MELBA'S ADVICE TO CLARA BUTT
(AND IT WASN'T 'BUTT OUT')

When Clara Butt was about to tour Australia,
Dame Nellie Melba is said to have advised her:
'Sing 'em muck. It's all they understand.'
Melba later denied it: 'Dame Clara didn't need to be told.'

FIVE 'OURS'

Our Glad ....Gladys Moncrieff (1892–1976) musical comedy star
Our Joan ....Joan Sutherland (1926–) opera singer
Our Kylie ....Kylie Minogue (1968–) singer, actress
Our Nicole ....Nicole Kidman (1967–) actress
Our Cate ....Cate Blanchett (1969–) actress

TWO LEADERS OF THE 9TH DIVISION
BETWEEN THE WARS

Leslie Morshead

Chosen by Monash to assist with staff work associated with repatriation to Australia of 1st AIF. Rose to command several brigades in interwar militia, while also rising to become Sydney Manager of Orient Steamship Line. Later led successful defence of Tobruk, developing doctrine of 'defence in depth', 'making the besiegers the besieged'.

George 'Mud Guts' Wootten

Attended first post-war course at Staff College, Camberley (other graduates included Gort and Alanbrooke). Received a 'B' pass. Final report included comment 'rides well'. Left regular army 1923 to become a lawyer but remained in militia. By 1939 weighed 20 stone (127 kg). 'Yet his massive bulk enclosed an extraordinarily prehensile brain and great mental stamina.'

Source: Gen. John Coates, *Bravery Above Blunder*, Oxford University Press, 1999

AUSTRALIANS OF THE YEAR

Year	Winner	Occupation
2005	Dr Fiona Wood AM	*Medical scientist and surgeon*
2004	Steve Waugh AO*	*Cricketer*
2003	Professor Fiona Stanley AC	*Scientist*
2002	Patrick Rafter*	*Tennis player*
2001	Lt General Peter Cosgrove AC MC	*Army officer*
2000	Sir Gustav Nossal AC CBE FAA FRS	*Scientist*
1999	Mark Taylor*	*Cricketer*
1998	Cathy Freeman*	*Runner*
1997	Professor Peter Doherty	*Scientist*
1996	Doctor John Yu AM	*Doctor*
1995	Arthur Boyd AC OBE	*Artist*
1994	Ian Kiernan OAM	*Environmentalist*
1993	No award given – award dating system changed	—
1992	Mandawuy Yunupingu	*Singer, teacher*
1991	Archbishop Peter Hollingworth AO OBE	*Archbishop*
1990	Fred Hollows AC	*Surgeon*
1989	Allan Border AO*	*Cricketer*
1988	Kay Cottee AO*	*Yachtswoman*
1987	John Farnham	*Pop singer*
1986	Dick Smith	*Businessman*
1985	Paul Hogan AM	*Comedian*
1984	Lois O'Donoghue CBE AM	*Aboriginal activist*
1983	Robert de Castella MBE*	*Runner*
1982	Sir Edward Williams KCMG KBE	*Chair, 1982 Brisbane Commonwealth Games Foundation*
1981	Sir John Crawford AC CBE	*Economist*
1980	Manning Clark AC	*Historian*
1979	Senator Neville Bonner AO	*Senator*
1979	Harry Butler CBE	*Naturalist*

Year	Winner	Occupation
1978	Alan Bond	*Businessman*
1978	Galarrwuy Yunupingu AM	*Aboriginal activist*
1977	Sir Murray Tyrall KCVO CBE	*Official Secretary to Governors-General*
1977	Dame Raigh Roe DBE	*Country Women's Association leader*
1976	Sir Edward 'Weary' Dunlop AC CMG OBE	*Surgeon*
1975	Sir John Cornforth AC CBE	*Scientist, Nobel Prize winner*
1975	Major General Alan Stretton AO CBE	*Head, Natural Disasters Organisation*
1974	Sir Bernard Heinze AC	*Conductor*
1973	Patrick White	*Writer*
1972	Shane Gould MBE*	*Swimmer*
1971	Evonne Goolagong Cawley AO MBE*	*Tennis player*
1970	Sir Norman Gilroy KBE	*Cardinal*
1969	The Rt Hon Richard Gardiner Casey Baron of Berwick, Victoria and of the City of Westminister KG GCMG CH	*Former Governor-General*
1968	Lionel Rose MBE*	*Boxer*
1967	The Seekers	*Musicians*
1966	Jack Brabham OBE*	*Racing car driver*
1965	Sir Robert Helpmann CBE	*Ballet dancer*
1964	Dawn Fraser MBE*	*Swimmer*
1963	Sir John Eccles AC	*Scientist, Nobel Prize winner*
1962	Alexander 'Jock' Sturrock MBE*	*Yachtsman*
1961	Dame Joan Sutherland OM AC DBE	*Opera singer*
1960	Sir MacFarlane Burnet OM AK KBE	*Scientist, Nobel Prize winner*

* Sports people

SENIOR AUSTRALIANS OF THE YEAR

Year	Winner	Occupation
2005	Antonio Milhinhos	*Philanthropist*
2004	Tehree Gordon	*Animal welfare worker*
2003	Bruce Campbell MBE	*Chair, 2002 Year of the Outback*
2002	No award	—
2001	Prof. Graeme Clark AO	*Developer, Bionic Ear*
2000	Prof. Freda Briggs	*Humanitarian*
1999	Slim Dusty	*Singer*

LOCAL HERO AWARD

Year	Winner	Occupation
2005	Ben Kearney	*Environmental campaigner*
2004	Donna Carson	*Crime victims advocate*
2003	Brian Parry AFSM	*Bushfire fighter*

YOUNG AUSTRALIANS OF THE YEAR

Year	Winner	Occupation
2005	Khoa Do	*Filmmaker*
2004	Hugh Evans	*Aid worker*
2003	Lleyton Hewitt*	*Tennis player*
2002	Scott Hocknull	*Scientist*
2001	James Fitzpatrick	*Rural health activist*
2000	Ian Thorpe*	*Swimmer*
1999	Bryan Gaensler	*Scientist*
1998	Tan Le	*Community activist*
1997	Nova Peris-Kneebone*	*Hockey player*
1996	Rebecca Chambers	*Concert pianist*
1995	Poppy King	*Businesswoman*
1994	Anna Bown	*Biology student*

1993	No award given – award dating system changed	—
1992	Kieren Perkins OAM*	*Swimmer*
1991	Simon Fairweather	*Archer*
1990	Cathy Freeman*	*Runner*
1989	Brenden Borellini	*Deaf and blind student*
1988	Duncan Armstrong*	*Swimmer*
1987	Marty Gauvin	*Computer entrepreneur*
1986	Simone Young	*Conductor*
1985	Deahnne McIntyre*	*Wheelchair athlete*
1984	John Sieben*	*Swimmer*
1983	Michael Waldock	*Blind volunteer Coast Guard monitor*
1982	Mark Ella*	*Rugby player*
1981	Paul Radley	*Novelist (see also Literary Scandals)*
1980	Peter Hill	*Quadriplegic athlete*
1979	Julie Sochacki	*Community service*

* Sports people

WASHING ESSENTIALS: 1914

Supplies needed for washing:
Starch; blue; chemicals for softening water, such as ammonia, borax, soda; soap: mild, medium and soft; chemicals for taking out stains, such as oxalic acid, salts of lemon.

Apparatus for drying clothes:
Clothes-post, two to four; props to hold up line, grooved and pointed; clothes-line like window-sash cord, best kind (should be kept in bag when not in use); clothes pegs; clothes peg bag or basket; soft cloths for cleaning line if it must be left outside.

Lady Hackett (ed.)
The Australian Household Guide, 1914

ARCHIBALD PRIZE WINNERS

Awarded annually by the Trustees of the Art Gallery of NSW to the best portrait, 'preferentially of some man or woman distinguished in Art, Letters, Science or Politics, painted by any artist in Australasia during the 12 months preceding the [closing] date . . .' Paul Keating once said that it was ridiculous to say Australians weren't interested in art: 'What other country has an annual barney over a portrait prize?'

Year	Winner	Painting
2005	John Olsen	*Self Portrait Janus-Faced*
2004	Craig Ruddy	*David Gulpilil, Two Worlds*
2003	Geoffrey Dwyer	*A portrait of Richard Flanagan*
2002	Cherry Hood	*Simon Tedeschi Unplugged*
2001	Nicholas Harding	*John Bell as King Lear*
2000	Adam Cullen	*Portrait of David Wenham*
1999	Euan MacLeod	*Self Portrait/Head like a Hole*
1998	Lewis Miller	*Portrait of Allan Mitelman No 3*
1997	Nigel Thomson	*Barbara Blackman*
1996	Wendy Sharpe	*Self Portrait – as Diana of Erskineville*
1995	William Robinson	*Self Portrait with Stunned Mullet*
1993/94	Francis Giacco	*Homage to John Reichard*
1992/93	Garry Shead	*Tom Thompson*
1991/92	Bryan Westwood	*The Prime Minister (Paul Keating)*
1990	Geoffrey Proud	*Dorothy Hewett*
1989	Bryan Westwood	*Portrait of Elwyn Lynn*
1988	Fred Cress	*John Beard*
1987	William Robinson	*Equestrian Self Portrait*
1986	Davida Allen	*Dr John Arthur McKelvey Shera*
1985	Guy Warren	*Flugelman with Wingman*
1984	Keith Looby	*Max Gillies*
1983	Nigel Thomson	*Chandler Coventry*
1982	Eric Smith	*Peter Sculthorpe*
1981	Eric Smith	*Rudy Komon*
1980	No award	—

Year	Winner	Painting
1979	Wes Walters	*Portrait of Philip Adams*
1978	Brett Whiteley*	*Art, Life and the Other Thing*
1977	Kevin Connor	*Robert Klippel*
1976	Brett Whiteley	*Self Portrait in the Studio*
1975	Kevin Connor	*The Hon Sir Frank Kitto, KBE*
1974	Sam Fullbrook	*Jockey Norman Stephens*
1973	Janet Dawson	*Michael Boddy*
1972	Clifton Pugh	*The Hon E. G. Whitlam*
1971	Clifton Pugh	*Sir John McEwen*
1970	Eric Smith	*Gruzman – Architect*
1969	Ray Crooke	*George Johnston*
1968	William Pidgeon	*Lloyd Rees*
1967	Judy Cassab	*Margo Lewers*
1966	Jon Molvig	*Charles Blackman*
1965	Clifton Pugh	*R. A. Henderson*
1964	No award	—
1963	J. Carrington Smith	*Professor James McAuley*
1962	Louis Kahan	*Patrick White*
1961	William Pidgeon	*Rabbi Dr I. Porush*
1960	Judy Cassab	*Stanislaus Rapotec*
1959	William Dobell	*Dr Edward MacMahon*
1958	William Pidgeon	*Mr Ray Walker*
1957	Ivor Hele	*Self Portrait*
1956	William Dargie	*Mr Albert Namatjira*
1955	Ivor Hele	*Robert Campbell Esq*
1954	Ivor Hele	*Rt Hon R. G. Menzies, PC, CH, QC, MP*
1953	Ivor Hele	*Sir Henry Simpson Newland, CBE, DSO, MS, FRCS*
1952	William Dargie	*Mr Essington Lewis, CH*
1951	Ivor Hele	*Laurie Thomas*
1950	William Dargie	*Sir Leslie McConnan*
1949	Arthur Murch	*Bonar Dunlop*
1948	William Dobell	*Margaret Olley*
1947	William Dargie	*Sir Marcus Clarke, KBE*

Year	Winner	Painting
1946	William Dargie	*L. C. Robson, MC, MA*
1945	William Dargie	*Lt-General The Hon Edmund Herring, KBC, DSO, MC, ED*
1944	Joshua Smith	*Hon Sol Rosevear, MHR, Speaker of the House of Representatives*
1943	William Dobell**	*Joshua Smith*
1942	William Dargie	*Corporal Jim Gordon, VC*
1941	William Dargie	*Sir James Elder, KBE*
1940	Max Meldrum	*Dr J. Forbes McKenzie*
1939	Max Meldrum	*The Hon G. J. Bell, Speaker of the House of Representatives*
1938	Nora Heysen	*Mme Elink Schuurman*
1937	Normand Baker	*Self Portrait*
1936	W. B. McInnes	*Dr Julian Smith*
1935	John Longstaff	*A. B. ('Banjo') Patterson*
1934	Henry Hanke	*Self Portrait*
1933	Charles Wheeler	*Ambrose Pratt*
1932	Ernest Buckmaster	*Sir William Irvine*
1931	John Longstaff	*Sir John Sulman*
1930	W. B. McInnes	*Drum-Major Harry McClelland*
1929	John Longstaff	*W. A. Holman, KC*
1928	John Longstaff	*Portrait of Dr Alexander Leeper*
1927	George W. Lambert	*Mrs Murdoch*
1926	W. B. McInnes	*Silk and Lace*
1925	John Longstaff	*Portrait of Maurice Moscovitch*
1924	W. B. McInnes	*Portrait of Miss Collins*
1923	W. B. McInnes	*Portrait of a Lady*
1922	W. B. McInnes	*Professor Harrison Moore*
1921	W. B. McInnes	*Desbrowe Annear*

* In 1978 Brett Whiteley also won the AGNSW's Wynne Prize (awarded for a landscape painting or figurative sculpture) for *Summer at Carcoar*, and Sulman Prize (awarded for a subject/genre painting or mural) for *Yellow Nude*: the only time one painter has won all three prizes in one year.

** In 1943 two artists who had entered their work sued on the grounds that the winner, *Joshua Smith* by William Dobell, was not a portrait but a 'caricature'. They lost, but Dobell had a nervous breakdown.

PLAY SCHOOL HOSTS

Christine Anu 2004–

Lorraine Bayly 1966–1996

Colin Buchanan 1992–1999

Simon Burke 1988–

Glenn Butcher 1997–2000

Sarah Chadwick 1991

Justine Clarke 2000–

Benita Collings 1969–1999

Merridy Eastman* 1985–1986

Teo Gebert 2003–

Trisha Goddard 1987–1999

Sofya Gollan 1991–

Anne Haddy 1966–1967

John Hamblin 1970–2000

Noni Hazlehurst....1978–2001

Joy Hopwood........1995–1997

David James 1994–2000

Darlene Johnson....1968–1969

Janet Kingsbury.....1969–1996

Jay Laga'aia 2000–

Deborah Mailman 2000–

Donald MacDonald 1966

Andrew McFarlane 2000–

Pauline McLeod 1991–

Angela Moore 1994–2000

Rhys Muldoon 2000–

Nicholas Opolski 1994

Karen Pang.................... 1998–

Matt Passmore 2002–

Philip Quast 1981–1996

Ken Shorter 1969–1970

Alister Smart 1966–1996

George Spartels 1986–1999

Don Spencer 1968–1996

Peter Sumner 1974

Monica Trapaga ... 1990–1998

Leah Vandenberg.......... 2000–

John Waters.......... 1972–1991

David Whitney 2002–

* Merridy Eastman later worked as a receptionist in a brothel. Her autobiography is entitled *There's a Bear in There (and He Wants Swedish)*.

Note: Many other actors have made guest appearances throughout the program's history.

Source: Play School

MEMBERS OF THE ROYAL SHAKESPEARE COMPANY WHO TOURED AUSTRALIA IN 1973 AND STAYED ON

Hugh Keays-Byrne (played 'The Toecutter' in *Mad Max*)
Ralph Cotterill (played 'Pop' in *Bad Boy Bubby*)

DIFFERENT REPUTATIONS IN AUSTRALIA AND OVERSEAS

Edward John Eyre, brave explorer or brutal oppressor?

In Australia: Edward John Eyre (1815–1901) explored the Flinders Ranges and Eyre Peninsula before setting out across the Nullarbor Plain in 1841 with a white overseer and three Aborigines. Two of the Aborigines killed the overseer and escaped with most of the party's supplies, leaving him to struggle towards Western Australia with little water or food. He and his companion Wylie finally made it into Albany in July 1841. The Royal Geographic Society awarded him its gold medal.

Overseas: In 1864 Eyre was appointed Governor of Jamaica. His actions in putting down the 1865 Morant Bay Rebellion, involving the execution of more than 400 black Jamaicans, led to controversy in England. Several attempts were made by prominent liberals, including John Stuart Mill and Herbert Spencer, to have him charged with murder, while his defenders included Thomas Carlyle, John Ruskin, Alfred Tennyson and Charles Kingsley. Eyre received a pension, but was never offered another post.

Samual Marsden: flogging parson or Christian pioneer?

In Australia: The Rev. Samuel Marsden (1764–1838) arrived in NSW in 1794, becoming senior Church of England clergyman in 1800. He was also a magistrate (as well as a successful farmer and businessman) and had a reputation for severity. Typically for evangelicals of the time, he had a virulent hatred of Roman Catholicism, which coloured his attitude to Irish convicts.

Overseas: But in New Zealand Marsden is remembered as the 'Apostle to the Maoris', whom he described as 'A very superior people in point of mental capacity'. On Christmas Day 1814 Marsden became the first person to preach the Christian gospel in New Zealand; the result of his long friendship with Ruatara, son of Te Pahi, the paramount Chief of Nga Puhi. The Maori revered Marsden for his protection of them against settlers' incursions.

Bligh: tyrant of the *Bounty* or strong governor of NSW?

Overseas: William Bligh (1754–1817) became notorious for his period as captain of HMS *Bounty*. In April 1789, on the return leg of a voyage to collect breadfruit plants from Tahiti, the crew mutinied and set Bligh and 18 loyal men adrift on a small boat. His excellent navigation and strong discipline enabled them to reach Timor in six weeks. A court martial (routinely required in the case of the loss of a ship) acquitted him of undue severity, but a campaign by the relatives of the mutiny's ringleader, Fletcher Christian, led to Bligh's reputation for cruelty which continues to this day.

In Australia: In Australia he is remembered as a hot-tempered but basically decent Governor (1806–1808), trying to enforce the law against a self-serving clique of present and former NSW Corps officers protecting their monopolies – the most prominent being John Macarthur* – before finding himself the victim of a second mutiny. This is the view put forward by H. V. Evatt in his *Rum Rebellion* (1938). However in *Man of Honour* (2003), Michael Duffy argues that the behaviour of Macarthur and the NSW Corps can only be understood with reference to the code of the gentleman: Bligh was no gentleman, not simply because of his background (and fondness for abusive language) but because his word could not be relied upon.

* See Great Ausralian Feuds, p. 159

MODELS WITH A SECOND CAREER

Imogen Bailey	*singer*
Megan Gale	*acting, has skincare range*
Bessie Bardot	*author, entrepreneur*
Kristy Hinze	*acting*
Elle Macpherson	*lingerie range*
Jodhi Meares	*swimwear range*
Tara Moss	*author*

MEMORABLE QUOTES FROM AUSTRALIAN FILMS

Mad Max (1979)
KID: *Hey, Mister! What happened to the car?*
BUBBA: *What do you think happened?*
KID: *Looks like it's been chewed up and spat out.*
BUBBA: *Perhaps it was the result of an anxiety.*

Mad Max 2 (1981)
TOADY: *The Lord Humungous, Warrior of the Wasteland, the Ayatollah of Rock and Rollah.*

Mad Max Beyond Thunderdome (1985)
DR DEALGOOD: *Right now, I've got two men, two men with a gut full of fear. Ladies and gentlemen, boys and girls . . . dyin' time's here!*

Muriel's Wedding (1994)
JOANIE HESLOP: *You're terrible, Muriel!*

Caddie (1976)
TED: *You've got class and beauty.*

Picnic at Hanging Rock (1975)
IRMA: *Waiting a million years – just for us.*

The Adventures of Priscilla, Queen of the Desert (1994)
BERNADETTE: *An Abba turd?*

Wake in Fright (1970)
JOCK CRAWFORD: *Can't remember when we last had a murder in the 'Yabba. Had a few suicides, though.*

The Castle (1997)
DARRYL KERRIGAN: *Tell 'em they're dreamin'!*

Romper Stomper (1992)
SONNY JIM: *We came to smash everything and ruin your life. God sent us.*

Babe (1995)
MICE: *Pork is a nice, sweet meat.*

The Adventures of Barry McKenzie (1972)
BARRY McKENZIE: *Now listen mate, I need to splash the boots. You know, strain the potatoes. Water the horses. You know, go where the big knobs hang out. Shake hands with the wife's best friend? Drain the dragon? Siphon the python? Ring the rattlesnake? You know, unbutton the mutton? Like, point Percy at the porcelain?*
BLANCHE: *I think he wants to go to the loo.*

COMMEMORATING P. L. TRAVERS

Both the town of Maryborough, Queensland, and the Sydney suburb of Ashfield lay claim to P. L. Travers, the author of the children's book *Mary Poppins* made famous by the 1960s Disney film. And both have put up statues in her memory: in Maryborough, where Travers was born Helen Lyndon Goff in 1899, a statue has been placed outside her former home; in Ashfield, where Travers lived from 1918 to 1924, a statue of Mary Poppins featured in a local park – until vandals wrecked it in 2005.

But other Australian towns have claims on Pamela and her creation, too. In Allora, Queensland, a Mary Poppins figure has pride of place on the verandah of her home from age three to seven. In Bowral, NSW, where she also spent part of her childhood, a Mary Poppins-themed plaza has been proposed.

Apparently there are no statues of either Mary or Pamela in Britain, where P. L. Travers wrote *Mary Poppins*, and where she lived from 1924 until her death in 1996.

SYDNEY'S NORTH SHORE PUBS BY MUNICIPALITY

'Local Option', the right of localities to exclude or limit bars or saloons, was a central plank of the temperance platform from the 1880s onwards and best demonstrated on Sydney's posh north shore, where just a handful of pubs operates across a population of some 275,000.

North Sydney
Crows Nest Hotel
North Sydney Hotel
Vibe (previously Rest) Hotel
Greenwood Hotel
Commodore Hotel
Kirribilli Hotel
Oaks Hotel

Lane Cove
Lane Cove Hotel

Willoughby
Willoughby Hotel
Hotel Charles
Northbridge Hotel
Great Northern Hotel
Artarmon Inn

Mosman
Buena Vista Hotel
Hotel Mosman

Ku-ring-gai
Greengate Hotel
Pymble Hotel

FICTIONALISED AUSTRALIAN PLACES

Fictional name	Real name	Novel	Author
Carringbush	Collingwood	*Power Without Glory*	Frank Hardy
Foveaux	Surry Hills	*Foveaux*	Kylie Tennant
Bundanyabba	Broken Hill	*Wake in Fright*	Kenneth Cook
Paradise East	East Roseville	*Riders in the Chariot*	Patrick White
Mullumbimby*	Thirroul	*Kangaroo*	D. H. Lawrence

*The fictional 'Mullumbimby' is of course not to be confused with the real Mullumbimby on the NSW north coast.

THE 12-METRE YACHT FORMULA

$$\frac{L + 2d - F + \sqrt{S}}{2.37} = 12$$

Where L = length in metres
d = girth difference (i.e. between skin girth and chain girth)
F = freeboard
S = sail area in square metres

DEBORAH MAILMAN'S FILMOGRAPHY to 2005

Film, TV series	Role
Radiance (1998)	Nona
Dear Claudia (1999)	Cathy
Bondi Banquet (1999)	Herself
Play School (2000–)	Herself
The Monkey's Mask (2000)	Lou
The Third Note (2000)	Tina
The Secret Life of Us (2001–2005)	Kelly Lewis
Black Chicks Talking (2001)	Herself
Rabbit-Proof Fence (2002)	Mavis

THE MOTTO OF THE *SYDNEY MORNING HERALD*

From its foundation in 1831 until 1847,
the *Sydney Morning Herald* featured this quotation
from Alexander Pope on its masthead:

'In moderation placing all my glory, while Tories
call me Whig – and Whigs a Tory.'

THE YIRRKALA BARK PETITION, 1963

TO THE HONOURABLE SPEAKER AND MEMBERS OF
THE HOUSE OF REPRESENTATIVES

IN PARLIAMENT ASSEMBLED.

The Humble Petition of the Undersigned aboriginal people of
Yirrkala, being members of the Balamumu, Narrkala, Gapiny,
Miliwurrwurr people and Djapu, Mangalili, Madarrpa,
MagarrwanaImirri, Djambarrpuynu, Gumaitj, Marrakulu, Galpu,
Dhaluangu, Wangurri, Warramirri, Naymil, Riritjingu, tribes
respectfully showeth.

1. That nearly 500 people of the above tribes are residents of the
   land excised from the Aboriginal Reserve in Arnhem Land.
2. That the procedures of the excision of this land and the fate of
   the people on it were never explained to them beforehand, and
   were kept secret from them.
3. That when Welfare Officers and Government officials came
   to inform them of decisions taken without them and against
   them, they did not undertake to convey to the Government in
   Canberra the views and feelings of the Yirrkala aboriginal people.
4. That the land in question has been hunting and food gathering
   land for the Yirrkala tribes from time immemorial: we were all
   born here.
5. That places sacred to the Yirrkala people, as well as vital to their
   livelihood are in the excised land, especially Melville Bay.
6. That the people of this area fear that their needs and interests
   will be completely ignored as they have been ignored in the past,
   and they fear that the fate which has overtaken the Larrakeah
   tribe will overtake them.
7. And they humbly pray that the Honourable the House of
   Representatives will appoint a Committee, accompanied by
   competent interpreters, to hear the views of the people of
   Yirrkala before permitting the excision of this land.
8. They humbly pray that no arrangements be entered into with any
   company which will destroy the livelihood and independence of
   the Yirrkala people.

And your petitioners as in duty bound will ever pray God to help you and us.

[Aboriginal language text follows.]

[STAMP]
I certify that this Petition
Is in conformity with the
Standing Orders of the
House

14/8/63   Clerk of the House

[Signatures]

Milirrpum

Djalalingba   Manunu

Daymbalipu   Larrakan

Dhayila   Wulanybuma

Dundiwuy   Wawunymarra

Dhuygala   Nyabilingu

Raiyin

[STAMP]

House of Representatives
RECORD 3023
14 August 1963

CLERK

BLOGGERS

Australia is at the forefront of web logging, or 'blogging'. A blog is a web application which contains periodic posts on a common webpage, serving as a publicly accessible personal journal for an individual. Political blogs, with comments on the news – and how it's reported – have exploded in popularity in recent years. Some prominent Australian bloggers include:

Right

Tim Blair ....http://timblair.net/
Bernard 'Slatts' Slattery ....http://www.slattsnews.
observationdeck.org/
Arthur Chrenkoff ....http://chrenkoff.blogspot.com/
'The Currency Lad' ....http://thecurrencylad.blogspot.com/
Adrian Neylan...http://jafablog.typepad.com/
man_of_lettuce/
'Stanley Gudgeon' ....http://bunyip.blogspot.com/
'Evil Pundit' ....http://evilpundit.com/
'Wogblog' ....http://wogblog.blogspot.com/
'Bilious Young Fogey' ....http://biliousyoungfogey.blogspot.com/
'Pre-whacked Snakes' ....http://www.whackingday.com/
'Bitchin Monaro Guide' ....http://drivelwarehouse.com/
monaro/index.php
'Dirk Thruster' ....http://arm-the-insane.blogspot.com/
Rafe Champion.................http://www.the-rathouse.com/index.html
'Yobbo' ....http://gravett.org/yobbo/index.php

Left

Tim Dunlop ....http://www.roadtosurfdom.com/
'Gianna' ....http://she-sells-sanctuary.blogspot.com/
Jozef Imrich ....http://amediadragon.blogspot.com/
'Gummo Trotsky' ....http://tugboatpotemkin.blogspot.com/
John Quiggin ....http://johnquiggin.com/
Gary Sauer-Thompson ....http://www.sauer-thompson.com/
Robert Corr ....http://www.redrag.net/

Note: Website addresses were correct at time of writing.

TO BOTTLE FRUITS

Let the fruit to be preserved be quite dry, and without blemish. Take a bottle that is perfectly clean and dry within, and put in the fruit in layers, sprinkling sugar between each layer, put in the bung, and tie bladder over, setting the bottles, bung downwards, in a large stewpan of cold water, with hay between to prevent breaking. When the skin is just cracking, take them out. All preserves require exclusion from the air. Place a piece of paper dipped in sweet oil over the top of the fruit; prepare thin paper, immersed in gum-water, and while wet, press it over and around the top of the jar; as it dries, it will become quite firm and tight.

From *Enquire Within Upon Everything*, 1894

STRENGTH OF AUSTRALIAN ARMED FORCES, 1901–2004

Year	RAN	Army	RAAF
1901		28 886	
1905		20 499	
1910		23 509	
1915	9 423	279 445	
1920	10 325	102 665	
1925	4 674	38 889	524
1930	4 475	27 454	1 242
1935	4 177	29 262	1 450
1940	11 600	91 802	32 083
1945	39 650	377 598	154 511
1950	15 195	32 779	9 594
1955	18 155	108 275	18 400
1960	18 414	59 714	16 178
1965	17 708	55 163	18 470
1970	19 472	77 829	24 151
1975	17 396	51 888	22 100
1980	16 961	32 321	22 249
1985	16 059	32 460	22 863
1990	13 404	27 298	19 770
1995	12 563	23 377	14 747
2000	12 717	24 677	13 535
2004	13 133	25 446	13 455

Sources: J. Grey, *A Military History of Australia*, 1999, and Australian Bureau of Statistics

WHY THE AUSSIE *ACACIA* IS CALLED 'WATTLE'

The earliest houses of the white settlers were constructed using the ancient technique of 'wattle and daub': branches such as those of acacia species were woven together on a frame and then daubed with mud. The name stuck.

AMERICANS PROMINENT IN
AUSTRALIAN LIFE

Charlie Brown....................Fashion designer originally from California

Freeman Cobb...................Founder of Cobb & Co. stagecoaches, 1853.

Bob Dyer ....*BP Pick-a-Box* quiz show host and big-game fisherman, 1940s–1970s.

The Foster Brothers
  (William and Ralph) ......Founders of Foster's brewery, 1887.

Hayes Gordon...................Actor and director, founder of Sydney's Ensemble Theatre, 1958.

Lee Gordon ....Sydney concert promoter, 1950s–60s.

Marcia Hines ....Singer and *Australian Idol* judge, came to Australia with *Jesus Christ Superstar* in which she played Mary Magdalene.

Livingston Hopkins ....*Bulletin* cartoonist, created 'The Little Boy at [or from] Manly' as a symbol of Australia, 1885.

Don Lane ....TV entertainer. His variety show *The Don Lane Show* ran for eight years from 1974.

Douglas MacArthur ....Supreme Commander, South-West Pacific Theatre, World War II, 1942–45.

King O'Malley ....Federation-era politician (claimed to be Canadian).

Norm Sanders ....Australian Democrat senator for Tasmania, 1984–90.

J. C. Williamson...............Actor theatrical manager, James Cassius Williamson stayed on in Australia after the success of his show *Struck Oil*. With a partner, he started a theatrical agency which became J.C. Williamson Ltd in 1911.

DAVID MORGAN

SOME MENTIONS OF AUSTRALIA IN FOREIGN FILM AND TV

Superman II (1980)
LEX LUTHOR: *I'm interested in a little piece of real estate . . . Australia!*

Butch Cassidy and the Sundance Kid (1969)
BUTCH: *I got a great idea where we should go next . . . Australia.*
SUNDANCE: *That's your great idea?*
BUTCH: *Oh, the greatest in a long line.*
SUNDANCE: *Australia's no better than here.*
BUTCH: *That's all you know.*
SUNDANCE: *Name me one thing better.*
BUTCH: *They speak English in Australia.*
SUNDANCE: *They do?*
BUTCH: *That's right, smart guy, so we wouldn't be foreigners. They got horses in Australia. And they got thousands of mountains you can hide out in. And good climate. Nice beaches. You could learn to swim.*
SUNDANCE: *No swimming! It isn't important. What about the banks?*
BUTCH: *They're easy. Easy, ripe, and luscious.*
SUNDANCE: *The banks or the women?*
BUTCH: *Once you've got one, you've got the other.*

Gilligan's Island (1964–1967)
'LOVEY' HOWELL: *We could give [the Professor] that little island we own in the Pacific.*
THURSTON HOWELL III: *Oh, you mean Australia?*

The Princess Bride (1987)
WESTLEY: *You've made your decision, then?*
VIZZINI: *Not remotely! Because iocaine comes from Australia, as everyone knows. And Australia is entirely peopled with criminals. And criminals are used to having people not trust them, as you are not trusted by me, so I can clearly not choose the wine in front of you.*

WESTLEY: *Truly, you have a dizzying intellect.*
VIZZINI: *Wait till I get going! [Pause] Where was I?*
WESTLEY: *Australia.*

THREE AUSTRALIAN CORNERS ...

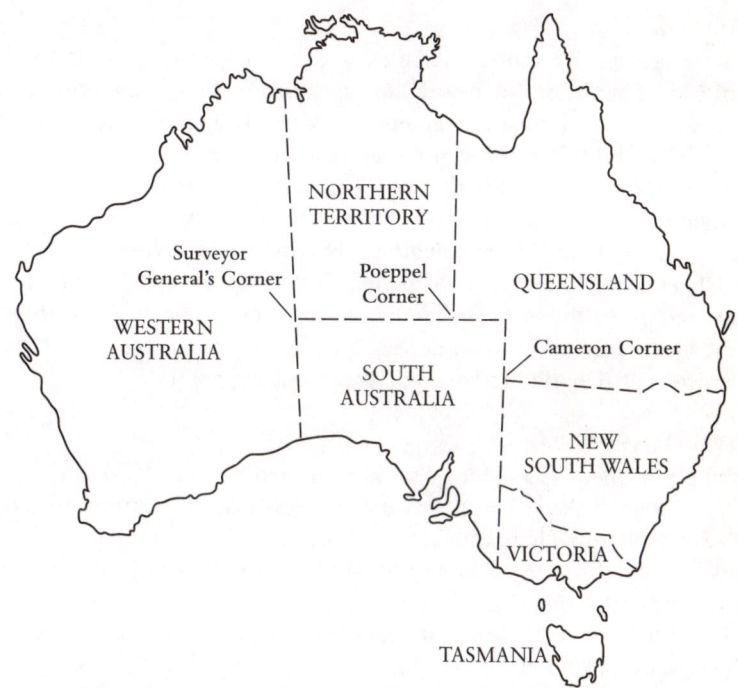

... AND TWO FENCES

The rabbit-proof fence: bisects WA; 1827 km long.
The dingo fence: world's longest fence at 5614 km; stretches from
SA to Qld, including the NSW borders.

AUSTRALIAN LITERARY HOAXES

Paul Radley

Aged 19, won the 1980 *Australian*/Vogel Award for writers aged under 35 for the novel *Jack Rivers and Me*, and was voted Australian of the Year in 1981. In 1996, he admitted it had been written by his middle-aged uncle Jack Radley.

'Ern Malley'

A poet created by James McAuley and Harold Stewart in 1944 to fool Max Harris, editor of the literary journal *Angry Penguins*, and to attack the modernist movement in poetry. They invented the dead poet 'Ern Malley', writing nonsensical poems under his name and sending them to Harris with a covering letter purporting to be from Malley's sister Ethel. Harris hailed them as works of genius, publising them in *Angry Penguins*. Eventually the truth came out and Harris was held up to ridicule. But McAuley and Stewart are now better-remembered for the Ern Malley poems than for anything they wrote under their own names. Sir Herbert Read, among others, claimed that they had unwittingly created great poetry.

Helen Darville

Winner of the 1995 Miles Franklin Award, the 1993 Australian/ Vogel Literary Award and the 1995 Australian Literature Society Gold Medal for *The Hand That Signed the Paper*. While she was undoubtedly the author, she wrote as 'Helen Demidenko', claiming to be of Ukrainian ancestry, and that the novel was based on her father's experience in World War II. In fact her ancestry was Anglo-Saxon. The novel was later republished under the name Helen Darville.

Norma Khouri

Wrote the 'memoir' *Forbidden Love* about living in Jordan, and about the 'honour killing' of her best friend, Dalia. After it had sold many copies in Australia, Malcolm Knox, Literary Editor of the *Sydney Morning Herald*, in 2004 disputed its authenticity and reported that she had grown up in Chicago from the age of three.

'B. Wongar'
A Serbian migrant, Streten Bosik, who came to Australia in the 1960s, and from 1978 onward wrote a series of novels and short story collections from an Aboriginal perspective, including *The Track to Bralgu*, *Raki*, *Dingoes Den* and *Last Pack of Dingoes*.

'Wanda Koolmatrie'
The pseudonym of Sydney cab driver Leon Carmen, whose 'memoir' *My Own Sweet Time* was written from the perspective of an Aboriginal woman.

AUSTRALIAN ADVERTISING SLOGANS
AND CATCHPHRASES

Slogan/Catchphrase	Product
Not happy, Jan!	Yellow Pages
You need Uncle Sam	Uncle Sam deodorant
When you're on a good thing, stick to it	Mortein fly spray
I feel like a Toohey's or two	Toohey's beer
The Big Australian	BHP
Beautiful one day, perfect the next	Queensland
Seven miles from Sydney and a thousand miles from care	Manly
M-E-N-T-H-O-I-D-S	Dr MacKenzie's Menthoids
You can feel them doing you good	Irish Moss
I like Aeroplane Jelly, Aeroplane Jelly for me	Aeroplane Jelly
Gone to Gowings	Gowings department store, Sydney
I can feel a XXXX coming on	Castlemaine XXXX beer
Don't argue – Hutton's is best	Hutton's smallgoods
A cup of tea, a Bex, and a good lie down	Bex
Holler for a Marshall	Marshall car batteries
We're happy little Vegemites	Vegemite
It's moments like these, you need Minties	Minties

PRIME MINISTERS' SCHOOLS

John Howard ....Canterbury Boys High School
Paul Keating ....De La Salle College, Bankstown
Bob Hawke...Perth Modern School
Malcolm Fraser ....Melbourne Church of England
Grammar School
Gough Whitlam ....Knox Grammar School
William McMahon ....Sydney Grammar School
John Gorton ....Sydney Church of England
Grammar School
('Shore'),
Geelong Grammar School
John McEwen ....Wangaratta State School
Harold Holt ....Wesley College, Melbourne
Robert Menzies ....Wesley College, Melbourne
Ben Chifley ....Patrician Brothers School, Bathurst
Francis Forde ....Christian Brothers College, Toowoomba
John Curtin ....St Ambrose's Primary School, Brunswick
Arthur Fadden ....Walkerston State School
Earle Page ....Sydney High School
Joseph Lyons ....Stanley State School
James Scullin ....Trawalla and Mount Rowan State Schools,
Ballarat
Stanley Bruce ....Melbourne Church of England Grammar School
William Morris Hughes ....Llandudno (Wales) Primary School
Andrew Fisher ....Crosshouse (Scotland) Primary School
Joseph Cook ....No formal schooling
George Reid ....Melbourne Academy (later called
Scotch College)
John Christian Watson ....Weston (New Zealand) School
Alfred Deakin ....Melbourne Church of England
Grammar School
Edmund Barton ....Fort Street High School,
Sydney Grammar School

PUMPKIN SCONES

Strongly associated with Flo Bjelke-Petersen, former senator and wife of the late Queensland premier, pumpkin scones are a tradition in that state. The following is an old Queensland recipe:

1½ cups SR flour
1 dessertspoon butter
1 tablespoon sugar
1 cup cold mashed pumpkin
½ cup milk

Rub butter into flour then stir in sugar. Add pumpkin and milk. Mix with knife. If mixture is too sticky, add more flour. Press out lightly on floured board then cut into scones. Bake in hot oven for 10–15 minutes or until golden.

TOP 10 THOROUGHBRED RACES
BY PRIZE MONEY

Race	Venue	Prizemoney
1. Melbourne Cup	Flemington	$4,150,000
2. Golden Slipper Stakes	Rosehill	$3,026,330
3. W. S. Cox Plate	Moonee Valley	$3,020,000
4. Doncaster Handicap	Randwick	$2,410,360
5. Caulfield Cup	Caulfield	$2,165,000
6. The BMW	Rosehill	$2,021,930
7. AJC Derby	Randwick	$1,912,860
8. AAMI Victoria Derby	Flemington	$1,257,000
9. 3YO Golden Rose	Rosehill	$1,021,825
10. AAMI Stradbroke Handicap	Eagle Farm	$1,020,000

FAMOUS 'AUSTRALIANS' ACTUALLY
BORN ELSEWHERE

Name	Born
Bee Gees	UK (and returned there)
Russell Crowe	NZ
Collette Dinnigan	NZ
Joe Dolce	US
Peter Finch	UK
Neil and Tim Finn	NZ
Rebecca Gibney	NZ
Mel Gibson	US
Nicole Kidman	US
Ted Mulry	UK
Olivia Newton-John	UK
Phar Lap	NZ
Bon Scott	UK
Rowena Wallace	UK
Naomi Watts	UK (long time resident in US)
Stevie Wright	UK
John Paul Young	UK

AUSTRALIAN STATE AND TERRITORY MOTTOES

ACT 'For the Queen, the Law and the People.'
NSW '*Orta recens, quam pura nites.*'
('Newly Risen, How Brightly You Shine.')
Queensland '*Audax at fidelis.*' ('Bold, Aye, and Faithful Too.')
Tasmania '*Ubertas et Fidelitas.*' ('Fertility and Faithfulness.')
Victoria 'Peace and Prosperity.'

The Northern Territory, South Australia and Western Australia have no mottoes on their coats of arms. However, before Western Australia was granted arms in 1969, it had an unoffical emblem featuring the black swan and a Latin pun, '*Cygnis Insignis*' ('Distinguished for Swans').

THE CURIOUS CONNECTION BETWEEN
TWO AUSSIE 'ICONS'

In Queensland in 1884, one Daisy O'Dwyer married a young stockman named Edwin Murrant. He was 19 and she was 25, though she claimed to be 21. It was a short-lived union – they separated within weeks of the wedding. Murrant later changed his name to Harry Morant, and became famous (or infamous) as '**The Breaker**'. Although they never divorced, Daisy married Jack Bates at Nowra in 1895 – still claiming to be 21. **Daisy Bates** has become part of Australia's folklore for her work with Aboriginal tribes.

THE SURRENDER OF THE *EMDEN*

After HMAS *Sydney*'s battle with the German ship *Emden* on 9 November 1914, *Sydney*'s Captain John H. Glossop sent his famous signal: '*Emden* beached and done for.' He then sent this letter to *Emden*'s Captain von Müller:

Sir,
I have the honour to request that in the name of humanity you now surrender your ship to me. In order to show how much I appreciate your gallantry, I will recapitulate the position.
   (1) You are ashore, 3 funnels and 1 mast down and most guns disabled.
   (2) You cannot leave this island, and my ship is intact.
In the event of your surrendering, in which I venture to remind you is no disgrace but rather your misfortune, I will endeavour to do all I can for your sick and wounded and take them to hospital.

> I have the honour to be,
> Sir,
> Your obedient Servant,
> John H. Glossop,
> Captain.

THREE FAMOUS AUSTRALIAN DOGS

Red Dog: during the 1970s this stray became well-known throughout the Dampier, WA, area, hitching rides on local buses.

The Dog on the Tuckerbox: at Gundagai, NSW, a statue commemorates a 1920s song about a dog that guarded his master's tuckerbox.

The dingo: tragically, in August 1980 a dingo took baby Azaria Chamberlain at Uluru National Park.

NOT FAIR DINKUM

You don't drink, you don't smoke, you don't go to the races. You don't live in the real world. You live in a government-tax-bludging society. You are a million words in search of an editor. You are a commissioner for the future style of person. You are not a real fair dinkum Aussie.

John Singleton on Phillip Adams

(The ad guru was commenting on journalist, commentator and former ad man Adams' support for regulation of television advertising in 1992)

SIX DECADES OF SUNDAY EVENING TV (SYDNEY)

26 November 1956

ABC	Seven	Nine
7.00: Sunday Magazine. 7.30: Olympic Games Highlights. 8.00: Fabian of Scotland Yard. 8.30: Life with Elizabeth. 9.00: Away from it All. 9:30: UNICEF film – Danny Kaye. 11.30: Programme Notes, Close.	7.30: Official Opening of Channel 7 – by the Postmaster-General, Mr C.W. Davidson. 7.45: Studio Variety Programme. 9.45: Film – "It's Folly to be Wise," Alistair Sim. 10.30: News.	6.30: Faith for Today. 7.00: News Magazine. 7.15: Johnny O'Connor. 7.30: Robin Hood. 8.00: What's My Line. 8.30: Our Miss Brooks. 9.00: This is the Life. 9.30: Olympic Games. 10.00: News and Weather.

3 December 1961

ABC	Seven	Nine
6.00: Lassie – "Sermon," John Provost, Jon Sheppodd and Gloria [Cloris?] Leachman, adventure. **6.25: This May Interest You** – Charity **6.30: The Cry Goes Up** – Documentary. **7.00: News and Weekend Magazine** **7.30: Boyd, Q.C.** – "Death on Tap," Michael Denison, Charles Leno, drama series (A). **8.00: An Age of Kings** – "Fall of a Protector" (Henry VI), historical drama. **9.00: Spotlight** – On Signe Drieyer. **9.30: American Musical Theatre** – "The Twenties – Musical Comedies," history. **10.00: The Last Chronicle of Barset** – "How Did He Get It?" B.B.C. drama series. **10.30: Epilogue** – "The Faithful In One Thing." (10.45: Close)	**6.00: Mr Magoo** – Cartoon series. **6.30: The Jack Benny Program** – "Death Row Sketch," Mamie Van Doren and Jack Benny, comedy series. **7.00: News and Newsreel** – Read by Kevin Sanders. **7.20: A.L.P. Election Talk.** **7.30: Anzac** – "Bardia, The First Battle," documentary series. **8.00: Revue 61** – Digby Wolfe comperes, with Helen Forest, the Revue 20, variety. **9.00: Sunday Theatre** – "Double Indemnity," Fred MacMurray, Barbara Stanwyck, Edward G. Robinson (A). **11.00: Talking Point** – Discussion chaired by Joe Gullett. **11.30: Reflection** – Bishop Goodwin Hudson. (11.35: Close.)	**6.00: TCN News and Newsreel.** **6.30: Disneyland** – "Jiminy Cricket Presents Bongo," Walt Disney, cartoon film. **7.30: Lawman** – "The Robbery," John Russell, Peter Brown, Peggy Castle, drama (A). **8.00: A.C.I. Theatre** – "The Adventures of Robin Hood," Olivia de Havilland, Errol Flynn, Claude Rains, Basil Rathbone, Ian Hunter, adventure. **10.00: Meet the Press** – David McNicoll. **10.30: Top of the Town** – Buster Fidess, Geoffrey Lenner, variety. (11.30: Close.)

5 December 1971

ABC	Seven
6.20: Why It Is So – J. Sumner Miller. 6.30: The Governor and JJ – Comedy. 6.55: Weather, News and Magazine. 7.30: All Gas and Gaiters – "The Bishop Has a Rest." Robertson Hare. 8.00: The Beggar's Opera – (A). Musical. 9.10: Wednesday's Child – Drama by Roger Marshall. Katherine Blake. 10.00: News and Weather. 10.10: Out in the Open – A look at the Open Air Campaigners organisation. 10.40: Never a Cross Road. (11.05: Close.)	6.00: News, Weather and "Sunday". 6.30: Riptide – "One Way to Nowhere." Clare Dunne, Norman Kay[e], Roger Ward. 7.30: Engelbert Humperdinck Show – Musical variety. With Caterina Valente, Don Knotts, singer Malcolm Roberts. 8.30: Academy Theatre – "Shadow on the Land." (A.O.) Premiere. Jackie Cooper, Carol Lynley, Janice Rule, John Forsythe, Marc Strange. 10.30: Playboy After Dark – Cabaret. 11.30: One Way. (12.00: Close.)

6 December 1981

ABC	Seven	Nine
6.00: Countdown. 6.55: News and Weekend Magazine. 7.40: Churchill and the Generals – (Rpt). Timothy West. 9.10: News and Weather. 9.20: Churchill and the Generals – Continued. 10.35: World of Music. (11.35: Close.)	6.00: News and Weather. 6.30: Wonderland Cove – "Crate Expectations." 7.30: Trapper John MD – (PGR) Pernell Roberts. 8.30: Whiffs (AO, 76). Comedy, Elliott Gould, Eddie Albert, Jennifer O'Neill. 10.40: Big League Soccer. 11.40: The Ropers (PGR). 12.20: Religious Program. (12.40: Close.)	2.30 – 6.30: Cricket – Benson and Hedges World Series Cup, Australia v Pakistan. Live from Adelaide. 6.30: News and Weather. 7.30: Lou Grant – (PGR) Ed Asner. 8.30: Movie – Oklahoma Crude (AO, 73, Rpt). George C. Scott. 10.30: Cricket – Highlights. 11.30: The Evil Touch (AO, Rpt). 12:00 – Movies (Rpts) beginning with Ten Rillington Place (AO, 71).

5 December 1971 (cont)

Nine	Ten
6.00: Safari to Adventure – Nature. **6.30: News and Weather.** **7.00: Disneyland** – "From All of Us to All of You." A Christmas Salute. **8.00: Mary Tyler Moore Show.** **8.30: The Odd Couple** – "Felix Gets Sick." **9.00: Sunday Night at the Movies** – "The Mind Benders." (A). Premiere. Dirk Bogarde. **10.55: Late News.** **11.05: Meet the Press.** **11.35: Silent Force** – Ed Nelson. **12.05: In Focus** – A program with a message. **12.35: Viewpoint.** (12.45: Close.)	**6.00: News and Weather.** **6.30: Wild Kingdom** – "Chincoteague Roundup" and "Lions of Gir Forest." **7.30: Room 222** – "I Hate You Silas Marner" and "Naked We Came Into the World." **8.30: Movie of the Week** – "The Sun Also Rises." Ava Gardner, Tyrone Power, Errol Flynn, Mel Ferrer, Eddie Albert, Robert Evans. **11.00: My Friend Tony** – "The Shortest Courtship." Karen Valentine. **12.00: Listen Hear!** (12.05: Close.)

6 December 1981 (cont)

Ten	SBS
6.00: News and Weather. **6.30: Young Talent Time.** **7.30: House Calls** – (PGR). **8.30: Movie** – Inside Daisy Clover (AO, Rpt, 66). Natalie Wood, Robert Redford. **11.00: That's Hollywood** (Rpt). **12.00: And Mother Makes Three** (Rpt). **1.00: Religious** (Rpt). (1.05: Close.)	**5.50: The Orphan.** (France). **6.20: Salto Mortale** – A circus family (Germany). **8.30: The Europeans** – documentary series (Italy). **8.30: Movie** – Hungarian Rhapsody and Allegro Brabaro (79). Gyorgy Cserhalmi. (Hungary) **11.30: S.C.O.O.P.** – (Rpt). Hosted by Xavier de Barcenas. (12.30: Close.)

1 December 1991

ABC	Seven	Nine
6.30: Brushstrokes – (Rpt). **7.00: News, Sport and Weather. 7.30: The River Kings** – (Final). Bill Kerr. **8.30: Sunday Stereo** – Don Giovanni. Australian Opera production. Jeffrey Black. (Simulcast ABC – FM). **11.20: Compass** – Missionaries **12.10: Hill Street Blues** – (AO). Daniel J. Travanti. **1.00: Tales from the Darkside** – (PGR). (1.45: Close.)	**6.00: News, Sport and Weather. 6.30: The Magical World of Disney** – The Journey of Natty Gann. **8.30: Movie** – Splash! (PGR, 84, Rpt). Tom Hanks, Daryl Hannah. **10.50: Motor Car Racing** – NASCAR and AUSCAR, from Calder Park. **12.30: NBC Sunday Today** – Topical.	**6.00: News, Sport and Weather. 6.30: Our World**: Islands of Refuge. The fauna of the Seychelles. **7.30: The Best of 60 Minutes** – (1991 Final). Yearly round-up. **8.30: Movie** – Merry Christmas, Mr Lawrence (AO, 83, Rpt). David Bowie, Tom Conti, Ryuichi Sakamoto, Jack Thompson. **11.00: News. 11.35: Cricket** – Highlights, First Test, Australia v India. **12.05: Moonlighting** – (PGR). **1.05: Movies.**

2 December 2001

ABC	Seven	Nine
6.10: Head Start – (Final). **7.00: News. 7.30: The Blue Planet** – Coasts. (Final.) **8.25: News. 8.30: Rising Stars: The 2001 Schools Spectacular. 10.00: Compass: Donald Horne. 10.35: Talking Heads: Playing Sandwiches** – (PG, Rpt). **11.10: Missing** – Presumed Alive – (M, Rpt). **12.35: High Treason** – (51, Rpt). Liam Redmond, Andre Morell.	**6.00: News. 6.30: Harry's Practice** – (Rpt). **7.00: Ground Force** – (Rpt). **7.30: Will and Grace** – (PG). Series return. **8.30: Movie** – Forget Paris (M, 95, Rpt). Billy Crystal, Debra Winger. **10.40: Movie** – Running Scared (M, 86, Rpt). Billy Crystal. **1.05: NBC Today.**	**6.00: News. 6.30: Cricket** – Third Test. Australia v New Zealand. Day three. Continues from WACA. **8.30: Movie** – Judge Dredd (M, 95, Rpt). **10.30: Newsbreak. 10.35: Movie** – Irresistible Force. **12.05: Star Trek: The Next Generation** – (PG). **1.05: Mini–series** – Barbara Taylor Bradford's A Woman of Substance (M, 83, Rpt).

1 December 1991 (cont)

Ten	SBS
6.00: News, Sport and Weather. 6.30 The Wonder Years – Comedy. 7.00: M*A*S*H* – (Rpt). Comedy. 7.30: Murder, She Wrote – (PGR). Angela Lansbury. 8.30: Movies – (AOs, Rpts). Bat 21 (88). Gene Hackman, Danny Glover. 10.40: Mother, Jugs and Speed (76). Bill Cosby, Racquel Welch. 12.40: World Sports – Highlights.	6.00: Hotline – Viewers' views. 6.30: World News and Weather. 7.30: Her Story – Women in Black. One in seven women in the UK has been widowed. (UK). 8.30: Telling Tales – The Sunset Gang. Harold Gould, Doris Roberts. (US). 9.30: The Secret Drawer. 10.30: The Movie Show. 11.00: Movie – Dark Times (AO, 81, Rpt). Jutta Lampe, Barbara Sukowa. (Germany). (12.45: Close)

2 December 2001 (cont)

Ten	SBS
6.00: Huey's TV Dinner. 6.30: The Crocodile Hunter – Steve Irwin. 7.30: Everybody Loves Raymond – (PG, Rpt). 8.00: What About Joan? – (PG). New series. 8.30: Movie – The Quick and The Dead (M, 95, Rpt). Sharon Stone, Russell Crowe, Gene Hackman. 10.40: News. 11.10: Sports Tonight. 11.40: The Power Tour – featuring truck racing and Nascar. 12.40: Happy Hour – (PG).	6.00: Sounds of the Seventies – (Rpt). Series return. (UK). 6.30: News. 7.00: World Sport. 7.30: A History of Britain – Burning Convictions 1500-1558. Simon Schama. (UK). 8.35: Evolution – The Evolutionary Arms Race. (US). 9.35: Masterpiece – Portrait of Barbara Hendricks. (France). 10.35: The Magic Flute – (PG, 75). (Sweden). 12.50: Hitler's Henchmen – (PG, Rpt). The Marshal: Hermann Goering.

MELBOURNE CUP WINNERS

Year	Horse	Weight kg (st.,lb. before 1972)	Jockey	Trainer
2004	Makybe Diva	55.5	G. Boss	D. J. Hall
2003	Makybe Diva	52	G. Boss	D. J. Hall
2002	Media Puzzle	52.5	D. Oliver	D. K. Weld
2001	Ethereal	52	S. Seamer	Ms. S. Laxon
2000	Brew	55.05	K. McEvoy	M. Moroney
1999	Rogan Josh	53.5	J. Marshall	J. B. Cummings
1998	Jezabeel	53	C. Munce	B. Jenkins
1997	Might and Power	56	J. Cassidy	J. Denham
1996	Saintly	55.5	D. Beadman	J. B. Cummings
1995	Doriemus	54.5	D. Oliver	D. L. Freedman
1994	Jeune	56.5	W. Harris	D. A. Hayes
1993	Vintage Crop	55.5	M. Kinane	D. Weld
1992	Subzero	54.5	G. Hall	D. L. Freedman
1991	Let's Elope	51	S. R. King	J. B. Cummings
1990	Kingston Rule	53	D. Beadman	J. B. Cummings
1989	Tawriffic	54	R. S. Dye	D. L. Freedman
1988	Empire Rose	53.5	T. K. Allan	L. K. Laxon
1987	Kensei	51.5	L. Olsen	L. J. Bridge
1986	At Talaq	54.5	M. Clarke	C. S. Hayes
1985	What a Nuisance	52.5	P. T. Hyland	J. F. Meagher
1984	Black Knight	50	P. Cook	G. M. Hanlon
1983	Kiwi	52	J. A. Cassidy	E. S. Lupton
1982	Gurner's Lane	56	L. Dittman	G. T. Murphy
1981	Just a Dash	53.5	P. Cook	T. J. Smith
1980	Beldale Ball	49.5	J. Letts	C. S. Hayes
1979	Hyperno	56	H. White	J. B. Cummings
1978	Arwon	50.5	H. White	G. M. Hanlon
1977	Gold and Black	57	J. Duggan	J. B. Cummings
1976	Van Der Hum	54.5	R. J. Skelton	L. H. Robinson
1975	Think Big	58.5	H. White	J. B. Cummings

Year	Horse	Weight kg (st.,lb. before 1972)	Jockey	Trainer
1974	Think Big	53	H. White	J. B. Cummings
1973*	Gala Supreme	49	F. Reys	R. J. Hutchins
1972	Piping Lane	48	J. Letts	G. M. Hanlon
1971	Silver Knight	8.9	R. B. Marsh	E. Temperton
1970	Baghdad Note	8.7	E. J. Didham	R. Heasley
1969	Rain Lover	9.7	J. Johnson	M. L. Robins
1968	Rain Lover	8.2	J. Johnson	M. L. Robins
1967	Red Handed	8.9	R. Higgins	J. B. Cummings
1966	Galilee	8.13	J. Miller	J. B. Cummings
1965	Light Fingers	8.4	R. Higgins	J. B. Cummings
1964	Polo Prince	8.3	R. Taylor	J. P. Carter
1963	Gatum Gatum	7.12	J. Johnson	H. G. Heagney
1962	Even Stevens	8.5	L. Coles	A. McGregor
1961	Lord Fury	7.8	R. Selkrig	F. B. Lewis
1960	Hi Jinx	7.1	W. A. Smith	T. H. Knowles
1959	MacDougal	8.11	P. Glennon	R. W. Roden
1958	Baystone	8.9	M. Schumacher	J. Green
1957	Straight Draw	8.5	N. McGrowdie	J. M. Mitchell
1956	Evening Peal	8	G. Podmore	E. D. Lawson
1955	Toparoa	7.8	N. Sellwood	T. J. Smith
1954	Rising Fast	9.5	J. Purtell	I. J. Tucker
1953	Wodalla	8.4	J. Purtell	R. Sinclair
1952	Dalray	9.8	W. Williamson	C. C. McCarthy
1951	Delta	9.5	N. Sellwood	M. McCarten
1950	Comic Court	9.5	P. Glennon	J. Cummings
1949	Foxzami	8.8	W. Fellows	D. Lewis
1948	Rimfire	7.2	R. Neville	S. Boyden
1947	Hiraji	7.11	J. Purtell	J. W. McCurley
1946	Russia	9	D. Munro	E. Hush
1945	Rainbird	7.7	W. Cook	S. Evans
1944	Sirius	8.5	D. Munro	E. Fisher
1943	Dark Felt	8.4	V. Hartney	R. Webster

Year	Horse	Weight kg (st.,lb. before 1972)	Jockey	Trainer
1942	Colonus	7.2	H. McCloud	F. Manning
1941	Skipton	7.7	W. Cook	J. Fryer
1940**	Old Rowley	7.12	A. Knox	J. A. Scully
1939	Rivette	7.9	E. Preston	H. Bamber
1938	Catalogue	8.4	F. Shean	A. McDonald
1937	The Trump	8.5	A. Reed	S. W. Read
1936**	Wotan	7.11	O. Phillips	J. Fryer
1935	Marabou	7.11	K. Voitre	L. Robertson
1934	Peter Pan	9.1	D. Munro	F. McGrath
1933	Hallmark	7.8	J. O'Sullivan	J. Holt
1932	Peter Pan	7.6	W. Duncan	F. McGrath
1931	White Nose	6.12	N. Percival	E. J. Hatwell
1930	Phar Lap	9.12	J. E. Pike	H. R. Telford
1929	Nightmarch	9.2	R. Reed	A. McAulay
1928	Statesman	8	J. Munro	W. Kelso
1927	Trivalve	7.6	R. Lewis	J. Scobie
1926	Spearfelt	9.3	H. Cairns	V. O'Neill
1925	Windbag	9.2	J. Munro	G. Price
1924	Backwood	8.2	P. Brown	R. Bradfield
1923	Bitalli	7	A. Wilson	J. Scobie
1922	King Ingoda	7.1	A. Wilson	J. Scobie
1921	Sister Olive	6.9	E. O'Sullivan	J. Williams
1920	Poitrel	10	K. Bracken	H. J. Robinson
1919	Artilleryman	7.6	R. Lewis	P. T. Heywood
1918	Night Watch	6.9	W. Duncan	R. Bradfield
1917	Westcourt	8.5	W. McLachlan	J. Burton
1916	Sasasnof	6.12	F. Foley	M. Hobbs
1915	Patrobas	7.6	R. Lewis	C. Wheeler
1914	Kingsburgh	6.12	K. G. Meddick	I. Foulsham
1913	Posinatus	7.1	A. Shanahan	J. Chambers
1912	Piastre	7.9	A. Shanahan	R. O'Conner
1911	The Parisian	8.9	R. Cameron	C. Wheeler

Year	Horse	Weight kg (st.,lb. before 1972)	Jockey	Trainer
1910	Comedy King	7.11	W. McLachlan	J. Lynch
1909	Prince Foote	7.8	W. McLachlan	F. McGrath
1908	Lord Nolan	6.1	J. Flynn	E. A. Mao
1907	Apologue	7.9	W. Evans	I. Earnshaw
1906	Poseidon	7.6	T. Clayton	I. Earnshaw
1905	Blue Spec	8	F. Bullock	W. Hickenbotham
1904	Acrasia	7.6	T. Clayton	A. E. Wills
1903	Lord Cardigan	6.8	N. Godby	A. E. Cornwell
1902	The Victory	8.12	R. Lewis	R. Bradfield
1901	Revenue	7.1	F. Dunn	F. Munro
1900	Clean Sweep	7	A. Richardson	J. Scobie
1899	Merriwee	7.6	V. Turner	J. Wilson (Jnr)
1898	The Grafter	9.2	J. Gough	W. Forrester
1897	Gaulus	7.8	S. Callinan	W. Forrester
1896	Newhaven	7.13	H. J. Gardiner	W. Hickenbotham
1895	Auraria	7.4	J. Stevenson	J. H. Hill
1894	Patron	8.3	H. G. Dawes	R. Bradfield
1893	Tarcoola	8.4	H. Cripps	J. Cripps
1892	Glenloth	7.13	G. Robson	M. Carmody
1891	Malvolio	8.4	G. Redfearn	J. Redfearn
1890	Carbine	10.5	R. Ramage	W. Hickenbotham
1889	Bravo	8.7	J. Anwin	T. Wilson
1888	Mentor	8.3	M. O'Brien	W. Hickenbotham
1887***	Dunlop	8.3	T. Sanders	J. Nicholson
1886	Arsenal	7.5	W. English	H. Rayner
1885	Sheet Anchor	7.11	M. O'Brien	T. Wilson
1884	Malua	9.9	A. Robertson	I. Foulsham
1883	Martini-Henri	7.5	J. Williamson	M. Fennelly
1882	The Assyrian	7.13	C. Hutchens	J. E. Savill
1881	Zulu	5.1	J. Gough	T. Lamond
1880	Grand Flaneur	6.1	T. Hales	T. Brown
1879	Darriwell	7.4	S. Cracknell	W. E. Dakin

Year	Horse	Weight kg (st.,lb. before 1972)	Jockey	Trainer
1878	Calamia	8.2	T. Brown	E. De Mestre
1877	Chester	6.12	P. Pigott	E. De Mestre
1876	Briseis	6.4	P. St Albans	J. Wilson
1875	Wollomai	7.8	R. Batty	S. Moon
1874	Haricot	6.7	P. Pigott	S. Harding
1873	Don Juan	6.12	W. Wilson	J. Wilson
1872	The Quack	7.1	W. Enderson	J. Tait
1871	The Pearl	7.3	J. Cavanagh	J. Tait
1870	Nimblefoot	6	J. Day	W. Lang
1869	Warrior	8.1	J. Morisson	R. Sevoir
1868	Glencoe	9.1	C. Stanley	J. Tait
1867	Tim Whiffler	8.11	J. Driscoll	E. De Mestre
1866	The Barb	6.9	W. Davis	J. Tait
1865	Toryboy	7	E. Cavanagh	P. Miley
1864	Lantern	6.3	S. Davis	S. Mahon
1863	Banker	5.4	H. Chifney	S. Waldock
1862	Archer	10.2	J. Cutts	E. De Mestre
1861	Archer	9.7	J. Cutts	E. De Mestre

*(1973): The author's only Melbourne Cup sweep win.
**(1936, 1940): Both 100–1 winners.
***(1887): Prime Minister Joseph Lyons's father lost his family's savings on the 1887 Melbourne Cup.

A SASHAY OF SUPERMODELS

Imogen Bailey
Megan Gale
Kristy Hinze
Elle Macpherson
Sarah Murdoch (née O'Hare)
Anneliese Seubert
Alyssa Sutherland
Gemma Ward

LEADERS OF THE LABOR PARTY WHO
NEVER BECAME PRIME MINISTER

Frank Tudor	1916–1922
Matthew Charlton	1922–1928
Herbert Vere Evatt	1951–1960
Arthur Calwell	1960–1966
Bill Hayden	1977–1983
Simon Crean	2001–2003
Mark Latham	2003–2005

LEADERS OF THE LIBERAL PARTY
(OR ITS PREDECESSORS)
WHO NEVER BECAME PRIME MINISTER

John Latham	1929–1931
Billie Snedden	1972–1975
Andrew Peacock	1983–1985, 1989–1990
John Hewson	1990–1994
Alexander Downer	1994–1995

WIGGLE SKIVVY COLOURS

Jeff ....purple
Murray..........red
Anthony ....blue
Greg..........yellow

TO FORWARD PHONECALLS
TO ANOTHER NUMBER

Dial*21, then the number, then #.
To turn the call forwarding off, dial #21#.

AUSTRALIAN NOBEL PRIZE WINNERS

William Henry Bragg and ....Physics, 1915
  William Lawrence Bragg
Howard Florey ....Physiology or Medicine, 1945
Frank Macfarlane Burnet....................Physiology or Medicine, 1960
John Eccles ....Physiology or Medicine, 1963
Patrick White...Literature, 1973
John Cornforth..Chemistry, 1975
Peter Doherty ....Physiology or Medicine, 1996

ARTS EXPATS: THE BIG FOUR

Robert Hughes ....*Art critic, historian*
Clive James..........................*Television presenter, critic, poet, novelist*
Germaine Greer ....*Feminist historian, literary academic, journalist*
Barry Humphries ....*Actor, cabaret performer*

TV WEEK KINGS AND QUEENS OF POP

Year	King of Pop	Queen of Pop
1969	John Farnham	Alison Durbin
1970	John Farnham	Alison Durbin
1971	John Farnham	Alison Durbin
1972	John Farnham	Colleen Hewett
1973	John Farnham	Colleen Hewett
1974	Jamie Redfern	Debbie Byrne
1975	Daryl Braithwaite	Debbie Byrne
1976	Daryl Braithwaite	Marcia Hines
1977	Daryl Braithwaite	Marcia Hines
1978	John Paul Young	Marcia Hines

Note: In 1967 Normie Rowe won *Go Set* magazine's popularity poll and was 'crowned' King of Pop on the *Go!!* television show that year and again in 1968. The next year this became the official *TV Week* King and Queen of Pop. At the 1996 ARIA Awards, Dave Graney jokingly proclaimed himself 'King of Pop' as he received his Best Male Artist Award, and the name stuck.

AUSTRALIAN AMERICA'S CUP
CHALLENGERS/DEFENDERS

Year	Yacht	Result
1962	*Gretel*	*Weatherly* won 4–1
1967	*Dame Pattie*	*Intrepid* won 4–0
1970	*Gretel II*	*Intrepid* won 4–1*
1974	*Southern Cross*	*Courageous* won 4–0
1977	*Australia*	*Courageous* won 4–0
1980	*Australia*	*Freedom* won 4–1
1983	*Australia II*	*Liberty* lost 4–3
1987	*Kookaburra III*	*Stars and Stripes* won 4–0

* *Gretel II* won the second race but was disqualified for an incident at the start.

THE AUSTRALIAN MIST CAT

Previously known as the Spotted Mist, it is the only breed of cat developed entirely in Australia. It was bred in 1977 by Dr Truda Straede, who combined Abyssinian, Burmese and domestic shorthair cats. The aim was to produce a spotted cat with a stable temperament which would adapt well to life indoors and not attack Australian native wildlife. It has a short, dense coat with darker spots on a lighter, 'misted' background. Recent breeding has seen the 'marbled' mist appearing, with marble-like swirls instead of spots. It is very tolerant of children.

VFL WINNERS 1900–04/
AFL LOSERS 2000–04

Winners of VFL Premiership	Losers of AFL Premiership
1900 – Melbourne	Melbourne – 2000
1901 – Essendon	Essendon – 2001
1902 – Collingwood	Collingwood – 2002
1903 – Collingwood	Collingwood – 2003
1904 – Fitzroy Lions	Brisbane Lions – 2004

GHOST TOWNS

Farina, SA
Kiandra, NSW
Kanowna, WA
Yerranderie, NSW
Cossack, WA
Ora Banda, WA
Cook, SA
Brooklyn Town, Vic
Gwalia, WA
Hammond, SA
Linda, Tas
Gormanston, Tas
Pillinger, Tas
Normanby, Qld
Newcastle Waters, NT

SOME (EUROPEAN) PLACE NAME CHANGES

Formerly known as:	Now known as:
Cape Everard	Point Hicks
Palmerston	Darwin
Mt Kosciusko	Mt Kosciuszko
Bearbrass	Melbourne
Emerald Hill	South Melbourne
Germanton, NSW	Holbrook
New Holland	Australia (mainland)
Van Diemen's Land	Tasmania
Blumberg, SA	Birdwood
Bushman's	Parkes
Ayers Rock	Uluru
Stuart	Alice Springs
Moreton Bay	Brisbane
Great Sandy Island	Fraser Island

NICKNAMES OF FAMOUS AUSTRALIANS

Alfie	Justin Langer
Bacchus	Rod Marsh
Biff	Mark Latham
Big Red	Phar Lap
Black Jack	John McEwen
Bomber	Kim Beazley
Chif	Ben Chifley
Diamond Jim	Jim McClelland
E.T.	Andrew Ettingshausen
Fatty	Paul Vautin
God	Gary Ablett
Jezza	Alex Jesaulenko
King	Wally Lewis
Ming	Sir Robert Menzies
Old Jack	Carbine
Plugger	Tony Lockett
Scud (or The Poo)	Mark Phillipousis
Skull	Kerry O'Keefe
Slats	Michael Slater
Tanglefoot	Max Walker
The Brick With Eyes	Glenn Lazarus
The Don	Sir Donald Bradman
The Flying Doormat	Bruce Doull
The King	Graham Kennedy and Kingston Town
The Lithgow Flash	Marjorie Jackson
The Macedonian Marvel	Peter Daicos
The Marrickville Mauler	Jeff Fenech
The Silver Bodgie	Bob Hawke
The Singing Budgie	Kylie Minogue
Thommo	Jeff Thomson
Thorpedo	Ian Thorpe
Weary	Sir Edward Dunlop

THE COMPLETE WORDS TO *ADVANCE AUSTRALIA FAIR*

Originally composed by Peter Dodds McCormick (1835–1916) and first performed in Sydney on St Andrew's Day, 1878, *Advance Australia Fair* was officially proclaimed as Australia's national anthem in 1984. The complete words are:

> *Australians all let us rejoice,*
> *For we are young and free;*
> *We've golden soil and wealth for toil,*
> *Our home is girt by sea;*
> *Our land abounds in Nature's gifts*
> *Of beauty rich and rare;*
> *In history's page, let every stage*
> *Advance Australia fair!*
> *In joyful strains then let us sing,*
> *'Advance Australia fair!'*
>
> *When gallant Cook from Albion sail'd,*
> *To trace wide oceans o'er,*
> *True British courage bore him on,*
> *Till he landed on our shore.*
> *Then here he raised Old England's flag,*
> *The standard of the brave;*
> *With all her faults we love her still,*
> *'Brittannia rules the wave!'*
> *In joyful strains then let us sing*
> *'Advance Australia fair!'*
>
> *Beneath our radiant southern Cross,*
> *We'll toil with hearts and hands;*
> *To make this Commonwealth of ours*
> *Renowned of all the lands;*
> *For those who've come across the seas*
> *We've boundless plains to share;*
> *With courage let us all combine*
> *To advance Australia fair.*
> *In joyful strains then let us sing*
> *'Advance Australia fair!'*

While other nations of the globe
Behold us from afar,
We'll rise to high renown and shine
Like our glorious southern star;
From England, Scotia, Erin's Isle,
Who come our lot to share,
Let all combine with heart and hand
To advance Australia fair!
In joyful strains then let us sing
'Advance Australia fair!'

Shou'd foreign foe e'er sight our coast,
Or dare a foot to land,
We'll rouse to arms like sires of yore
To guard our native strand;
Brittannia then shall surely know,
Beyond wide ocean's roll,
Her sons in fair Australia's land
Still keep a British soul.
In joyful strains the let us sing
'Advance Australia fair!'

Note: Only verses one and three are usually sung today. When the song became the national anthem, some changes were made to McCormick's original lyrics to satisfy the new fashion for political correctness:

• verse 1, line 1: 'Australia's sons let us rejoice' became 'Australians all let us rejoice'

• verse 3, line 3: 'To make this youthful Commonwealth' became 'To make this Commonwealth of ours'

• verse 3, line 5: 'For loyal sons beyond the seas' became 'For those who've come across the seas'

Many Australians find the words 'girt by sea' embarrassing. Oddly, they seem to have no problem with 'joyful strains'.

It is possible to sing the words of *Advance Australia Fair* to the tune of the *Gilligan's Island* theme, and vice versa. And for a really stirring effect, try singing them to the Jimmy Barnes classic *Working Class Man*.

AUSTRALIAN-BASED ARMED FORCES
THAT HAVE SERVED OVERSEAS

New Zealand Wars..1860–1872
Sudan 1885
Boer War 1899–1902
Boxer Rebellion..1900–1901
First World War..1914–1918
Second World War...1939–1945
British Commonwealth Occupation Forces, Japan 1945–1951
UN Good Offices Commission [Indonesia]......................1947–1949
UN Commission for Indonesia 1949–1951
UN Special Commission on the Balkans 1947–1952
UN Military Observer Group in India and Pakistan 1950–1985
UN Commission on Korea 1950
UN Command Military Assistance Commission [Korea] ...1950–1956
Malayan Emergency 1950–1960
UN Truce Supervision Organisation [Sinai] 1956–
UN Operation in the Congo 1960–1961
UN Temporary Executive Authority [West Irian] 1962
Vietnam War 1962–1972
UN Yemen Observation Mission 1963
UN Force in Cyprus 1964–
Indonesian 'Confrontation' with Malaysia 1964–1966
UN India–Pakistan Observation Mission.........................1965–1966
UN Disengagement Observer Force [Syria] 1974
Second UN Emergency Force [Sinai]...............................1976–1979
Commonwealth Monitoring Force [Zimbabwe] 1979–1980
Multinational Force and Observers [Sinai] 1982–
Commonwealth Military Training Team – Uganda..........1982–1984
UN Iran–Iraq Military Observer Group 1988–1990
UN Chemical Warfare Investigation Team......................1984–1987
UN Transition Assistance Force [Namibia]......................1989–1990
UN Border Relief Operation [Cambodia] 1989–1993
UN Mine Clearance Training Team................................1989–1993
First Maritime Interception Force....................................1990–1991
Multinational Forces in Iraq–Kuwait 1991

Second Maritime Interception Force 1991–
UN Mission for the Referendum in Western Sahara 1991–1994
UN Special Commission [Iraq] 1991–
UN Advance Mission in Cambodia 1991–1992
Operation Provide Comfort 1991
UN Transitional Authority in Cambodia 1992–1993
UN Protection Force [former Yugoslavia].......................1992–1995
NATO Stabilisation Force in Bosnia................................1995–
First UN Operation in Somalia 1992–1993
Unified Task Force in Somalia 1992–1993
Second UN Operation in Somalia....................................1993–1994
UN Assistance Mission in Rwanda..................................1994–1995
UN Operation in Mozambique...1994–1995
South Pacific Peacekeeping Force [Bougainville].............1994
Multinational Force [Haiti] 1994–1995
UN Mission for the Verification of Human Rights 1997–
  in Guatemala
Truce Monitoring Group [Bougainville] 1997–1998
Peace Monitoring Group [Bougainville] 1998–
UN Assistance Mission in East Timor.............................1999–
Coalition Force in Afghanistan.......................................2001–2004
Coalition Force in Iraq 2003–
Solomon Islands Peacekeeping Force 2003–
Humanitarian Assistance [Indian Ocean tsunami] 2004–

ORIGINAL RAILWAY GAUGES

Victoria..5 feet 3 inches
NSW...4 feet 8½ inches
Qld, WA, SA, Tasmania ....3 feet 6 inches

There was no standard-gauge rail link between Melbourne and
Sydney until 1962, while the standard-gauge transcontinental
railway between Sydney and Perth had to wait till 1970. Today,
the 4 feet 8½ inch standard gauge connects Brisbane, Sydney,
Melbourne, Perth, Alice Springs and Darwin.

GREAT MOMENTS IN AUSTRALIAN FASHION

1948 'New Look' comes to Australia with the first complete Dior collection ever to be shown outside Paris at David Jones, Sydney.

1961 Woman ordered off Bondi Beach for wearing 'revealing' swimming costume. Subsequent Les Tanner cartoon 'Get off the beach! You look obscene.' wins Walkley Award.

1965 Jean Shrimpton wears mini skirt, no gloves, no hat to Melbourne Cup.

1971 Sonia McMahon wears a white split-to-the-thigh gown to a White House dinner in honour of her husband, Prime Minister William McMahon.

1995 Lizzie Gardiner accepts Best Costume Design Oscar for *The Adventures of Priscilla, Queen of the Desert*, wearing a dress made out of American Express Gold Cards. Host David Letterman quips 'Lizzie Gardiner's dress has just expired.'

1995 Collette Dinnigan becomes the first Australian-based designer to mount a full-scale ready to wear parade in Paris.

HOW TO WASH A CHOOK

First, see that everything required is at hand before commencing. It is most inconvenient to stop with a well-lathered fowl in your hands to search for some more water or some other requirement. Use three troughs that will hold at least five or six gallons each, some good quality white soap, a dipper of melted soap that has been shredded into hot water, a supply of hot, soft water, a rinsing bowl, several clean towels, a warm fire, and a drying pen, preferably fitted with a perch, and having an open front. Fill the first two tubs with hot water, that is, cool enough to comfortably immerse the hands in, and the third with water just sufficiently warmed to take the chill off. In washing white birds, the blue bag can, with advantage, be dashed into the third tub, but don't overdo it. Strain the melted soap into the first tub and whisk the water about till it is covered with a lather.

Poultry in Australia, 1934

FALLEN JOCKEYS

Annually, between 25 and 40 per cent of all jockeys in Australia suffer a significant injury. On average, two have been killed on Australian racecourses and training tracks every year since records began. A memorial to Australian jockeys who have lost their lives while riding was unveiled at Caulfield Racecourse on National Jockey Celebration Day, 5 March 2005. Just over a week later, Gavin Lisk and Adrian Ledger were killed on consecutive days.

Name	Venue	Year	Name	Venue	Year
G. Marsden	Homebush	1847	J. Sheehan	Donald	1895
W. C. Wilson	Casino	1859	J. Felstead	Wagga Wagga	1895
J. Morrison	Flemington	1878	J. Callaghan	St Arnaud	1895
W. Boyd	Flemington	1879	H. Cusdin	Aspendale	1895
J. Breen	Adelaide	1879	E. Hampton	Coopers Creek	1895
J. Clark	Randwick	1880	C. Merry	Ballarat	1895
J. Hunt	Geelong	1881	C. Lewis	Caulfield	1895
G. Dodd	Flemington	1881	T. Gardiner	Kensington	1897
A. Fartch	Mt Gambier	1881	P. Hussey	Adelaide	1897
P. Carey	Hobart	1882	E. Wilson	Murrumbidgee	1897
J. Hayes	Mt Gambier	1882	C. O'Connor	Dunkeld	1897
A. McInnes	Flemington	1883	J. Leek	Caulfield	1898
R. Rowe	Randwick	1885	J. Laverty	Mentone	1898
R. Heath	Randwick	1885	B. Grey	Moe	1898
J. Elliot	Roseberry	1885	W. Rheece	Randwick	1899
J. Dyer	Gunbower	1885	W. Fernie	Kynnumboon	1899
D. Nicholson	Caulfield	1885	R. Bennison	Melbourne	1899
J. Cree	Flemington	1886	J. Hayes	Caulfield	1899
J. Williams	Flemington	1887	J. Fitzgerald	Elwick	1899
J. Hickey	Warrnambool	1887	J. Williams	Warrnambool	1900
A. Robertson	Randwick	1888	H. Dawes	Flemington	1900
A. Newlands	Bendigo	1889	T. Dean	Moonee Valley	1901
P. Strickland	Ascot, Qld	1890	J. Evans	Coolgardie	1901
G. Bell	Caulfield	1890	R. Manning	Flemington	1902
E. Farquarson	Caulfield	1890	H. Underwood	Flemington	1902
A. Watson	Moonee Valley	1890	E. Kennedy	Flemington	1902
R. Carey	Trentham	1891	J. Farrell	Ascot, WA	1903
C. Eastham	Flemington	1891	E. Watson	Geelong	1903
T. Williams	Dandenong	1892	T. Gibson	Burrumbeet	1905
J. Coe	Morphettville	1892	M. Mooney	Caulfield	1905
T. Vanevery	Sandown	1893	G. Connors	Sandy Creek	1905
T. Corrigan	Caulfield	1894	P. Regan	Moorefield	1906
P. McGowan	Flemington	1894	A. Windsor	Bulong	1906
M. Bourke	Flemington	1894	W. Skelton	Ascot, WA	1907
T. Manifold	Rockbank	1895	T. Hogan	Moonee Valley	1907

Name	Venue	Year
F. Croker	Flemington	1907
A. Carter	Morphettville	1907
L. McDougall	Ascot, WA	1908
J. Kent	Ascot, WA	1908
F. Hayhoe	Flemington	1908
T. Clayton	Rosehill	1909
S. Smith	Adelaide	1909
G. Howard	Randwick	1909
W. Powell Jnr	Coolgardie	1910
Rob Sutherland	Morphettville	1910
G. Watson	Ballan	1910
J. Johnson	Caulfield	1911
H. Holmes	Oakbank	1911
A. Percival	Ascot, WA	1911
R. Cherrington	Ascot, WA	1912
B. Williamson	Timboon Park	1912
C. Berglund	Cannington Park	1913
W. H. Smith	Rosehill	1914
R. Jaques	Morphettville	1914
J. Nicholls	Moonee Valley	1914
J. Mason	Oakbank	1914
B. Casey	Mentone	1914
A. Panowit	Adelaide	1914
J. Edwards	Epsom	1916
C. Jackson	Helena Vale	1917
A. Clarke	Moonee Valley	1917
W. Lawson	Merredin	1919
J. Tucker	Eagle Farm	1919
C. Diedrick	Halls Creek	1919
J. O'Reilly	Moonee Valley	1920
T. Walker	Mitta Mitta	1921
S. Wade	Cannington Park	1921
A. Martinez	Flemington	1921
S. Buckley	Goodooga	1922
N. Burrows	Ascot, WA	1922
L. Gray	Randwick	1922
W. Percival	Cannington Park	1924
T. Hamill	Mowbray	1924
J. Halden	Randwick	1924
F. Straker	Cannington Park	1924
F. Pearce	Elwick	1924
E. Sleight	Belmont, WA	1924
A. Renny	Fitzroy	1924
L. Butler	Cannington Park	1925
A. Donaldson	Eagle Farm	1925
W. Hibberd	Caulfield	1926
J. Bullock	Moonee Valley	1926

Name	Venue	Year
C. Boyd	Caulfield	1926
A. Todd	Ascot, WA	1926
A. Siefkin	Ascot, WA	1926
P. Dinsale	Caulfield	1927
N. McKinnon	Randwick	1927
J. Welsh	Redan	1928
G. Kenny	Warrnambool	1928
A. Skirving	Moonee Valley	1928
R. Tait	Broken Hill	1929
R. Gould	Caulfield	1929
R. Ellis	Mentone	1929
P. O'Hanlon	Caulfield	1929
H. Cairns	Moonee Valley	1929
E. Roberts	Belmont	1929
R. Townsend	Mentone	1930
K. Scott	Bittern	1930
K. McKenzie	Victoria Park	1930
J. Hughes	Wagga Wagga	1930
H. Martin	Gosford	1930
E. Olsen	Belmont	1930
R. Fuller	SA	1931
L. McNulty	Flemington	1931
J. Troy	Randwick	1931
H. Saw	Fitzroy	1931
F. Richardson	SA	1931
D. Hanrahan	Hampden	1931
W. Plumb	Qld	1932
P. Hynes	Vic	1932
W. Coates	Moonee Valley	1933
S. Lace	Ascot, Qld	1933
P. Spence	Eight Mile Plains	1933
J. Stubbs	Caulfield	1933
D. Morris	Randwick	1933
C. Penfold	Goodwood, WA	1933
J. Watson	Mowbray	1934
H. McKinnon	NSW	1934
C. Chapman	Whitton	1934
A. Knowles	Randwick	1934
A. Johnson	Oakbank	1934
A. Goddard	Ascot, Qld	1934
T. Lynch	Flemington	1935
R. Reed	Caulfield	1935
H. Davies	WA	1935
G. Oliver	Flemington	1935
E. Hammer	Hamilton	1935
D. McGrath	Bairnsdale	1935
A. Clark	Albury	1935

Name	Venue	Year
E. Meredith	Moonee Valley	1936
R. Morris	NSW	1937
M. Papworth	Randwick	1937
J. Moore	Singleton	1937
E. Johnson	Flemington	1937
C. Badger	Moonee Valley	1937
W. Lee	Moonee Valley	1938
S. Kite	Morphettville	1938
R. Wilson	Morphettville	1938
K. Voitre	Moonee Valley	1938
W. Newton	Flemington	1939
W. Elliott	Caulfield	1939
L. Sampson	Rosebrook	1939
K. Farrell	Mt Gambier	1939
J. Healey	NSW	1939
G. McMahon	Terang	1939
W. Lappin	Randwick	1940
J. Raven	Murray Bridge	1940
W. Shipton (Jnr)	Qld	1941
R. Harris	Cobar	1941
R. Fleming	Flemington	1941
M. O'Sullivan	Unknown	1941
L. Abrahams	Melbourne	1941
G. Jordan	Elwick	1941
C. Middlemiss	Unknown	1942
E. O'Donnell	Rosehill	1943
V. Courtney	Flemington	1944
V. Latham	Sydney	1945
W. Foley	Geelong	1946
W. Chadwick	Sydney	1946
J. Duncan	Randwick	1946
J. Newnham	Warrnambool	1947
J. Baggs	Bunbury	1947
R. Roberts	Victoria Park	1948
R. Pratt	NSW	1948
R. Goodwin	The Oaks, NSW	1948
R. Barry	Moonee Valley	1948
J. Crilley	Flemington	1948
C. Jarman	Warrnambool	1948
T. McInerney	Morphettville	1949
L. Tolay	Doomben	1949
J. Moyes	Morphettville	1949
H. McDonald	Goulburn	1949
J. Scudamore	Kyneton	1950
P. Duller	Morphettville	1951
M. Schmirer	Orange	1951
D. Fullarton	Flemington	1951

Name	Venue	Year
A. Wood	Boggabri	1951
M. Eascott	Rosehill	1952
L. McKee	Tasmania	1952
K. Knobel	Qld	1952
C. Knobb	Kembla Grange	1952
T. Maddern	Streaky Bay	1954
R. Gardener	Mentone	1954
K. Norrie	Glen Innes	1954
D. McLean	Oakbank	1954
J. Molloy	Numurkah	1955
O. Nicholls	Hamilton	1956
F. Dean	Mt Gambier	1956
M. Jessup	Oakbank	1957
M. Gray	Albury	1957
K. Jessup	Morphettville	1957
H. Toomer	Kyneton	1957
D. Barclay	Albury	1957
W. Campbell	Brewarrina	1958
T. Alvos	Orange	1958
Ross Sutherland	Gosford	1958
L. Smith	Cowra	1958
R. Phillips	Rosehill	1959
K. Grady	Armidale	1959
J. Vasil	Bacchus Marsh	1959
K. Ford	Caulfield	1960
J. Scarlett	New Delhi, India	1960
I. Cluff	Caulfield	1961
B. Shaw	Stawell	1961
R. Minter	Gympie	1962
N. Sellwood	Maison Lafitte, France	1962
E. Cox	Elwick	1962
A. Gallagher	Bourke	1962
R. James	Canterbury	1963
K. Hales	Epsom	1964
G. Aistrope	Belmont	1965
C. Kelly	Glen Innes	1967
A. Jones	Mt Isa	1967
R. Baker	Southport	1968
J. Marshall	Bunbury	1969
I. Roberts	Warialda	1970
W. Bell	Oakey	1971
A. Martin	Canberra	1972
S. Cassidy	Randwick	1974
P. Sykes	Warracknabeal	1975
A. Connor	Grafton	1975
S. Bundy	Randwick	1976

Name	Venue	Year			
P. Schumacher	Grafton	1976	N. Barker	Randwick	1993
W. Stradling	Bundaberg	1977	K. Russell	Rosehill	1993
R. Oliver	Kalgoorlie	1978	B. Howarth	Unknown	1993
M. Eveleigh	Quirindi	1980	H. McNeich	Allman Park	1996
D. Green	Rosehill	1980	D. Wilkes	Toowoomba	1996
C. Ayton	Scone	1980	C. Ericson	Kumbla	1996
K. Layton	Mornington	1981	W. Barnes	Flinton	1998
L. Lawson	Seymour	1982	P. John	Kalgoorlie	1998
A. Winch	Queanbeyan	1982	L. Goodwin	Roma	1998
G. Callander	Flemington	1983	J. Flanagan	Caulfield	1998
E. Savage	Appin	1983	D. Beckett	Ascot, WA	1998
C. Hanson	Mowbray	1983	B. Duggan	Mundijong	1999
J. Gray	Bordertown	1984	A. Gilbert	Benalla	2001
C. Cepero	Wagga Wagga	1984	J. Oliver*	Belmont	2002
W. Stevens	Geelong	1985	M. Goring	Tatura	2003
J. Spargo	Ayr	1985	N. Botica	Landor	2004
I. Neilson	Lismore	1988	A. Chan	Carnarvon	2004
C. Wake	Ascot, WA	1988	G. Lisk	Moe	2005
M. Johnston	Ballarat	1989	A. Ledger	Orange	2005
A. Yohey	Corbould Park	1989	W. Michaelson	Mowbray	Unknown
P. Birchell	Taree	1990	W. Curran	Mowbray	Unknown
D. Burns	Tamworth	1991	W. Cox	Mowbray	Unknown
L. Crook	Doomben	1992	R. Underwood	Mowbray	Unknown
			R. Kinsman	Randwick	Unknown

* A week after Jason Oliver's death, his brother Damien rode Media Puzzle to victory in the 2002 Melbourne Cup.

GREAT AUSTRALIAN LIBEL CASES

Peter and Tanya Costello, Tony and Margaret Abbott
The senior Liberal Party figures and their wives successfully sued Bob Ellis' publisher over his 1997 book *Goodbye Jerusalem*.

Jason Donovan
In 1992 the singer–actor successfully sued *The Face* magazine in Britain for libel over allegations that he was homosexual.

Andrew Ettingshausen
The rugby league player successfully sued the women's magazine *HQ* for giving the impression that he had permitted a photograph to be taken of his genitals, which *HQ* had published.

John Marsden

The Sydney solicitor and former head of the NSW Law Society successfully sued Channel Seven over a 1996 *Witness* and *Today Tonight* story alleging that he'd had sexual encounters with underage boys in the 1970s.

Mt Druitt High School students

Mount Druitt High School students successfully sued the Sydney *Daily Telegraph* for its 1997 front page story, 'The Class We Failed', which detailed the poor performance of the school in the Higher School Certificate.

Leo Schofield

The *Sydney Morning Herald* food critic was successfully sued for a 1980s restaurant review in which he complained about a lobster being overdone.

Pauline Hanson

The then Independent member of Federal Parliament and later leader of the One Nation Party sued the ABC in 1997 when radio station Triple J played the 'Pauline Pantsdown' song, *I'm a Backdoor Man*. It contained samples of her voice re-edited to make her seem to be saying 'I am a homosexual'. The court ordered that the song not be played again.

Harry Seidler

The Sydney architect sued over a Patrick Cook cartoon in the *National Times* in 1982. The cartoon, captioned 'Harry Seidler Retirement Park', showed elderly people encased in slabs of concrete with food being passed in through a slit on one side and faeces being removed from the other. Seidler was unsuccessful. The cartoon was deemed to be an honest opinion under the defence of fair comment.

Ellen Wren

The wife of John Wren (1871–1953), a multi-millionaire business-man and ALP power broker, had author Frank Hardy arrested and charged with criminal libel in 1950 over his novel *Power Without Glory*, claiming that the character of 'Nellie West', who has an adulterous affair, was based on her. Hardy was eventually freed.

AUSTRALIAN GEOGRAPHIA

In WA the sun can be seen to *rise* out
  of the sea at: ....Cape Naturaliste

In NSW the sun can be seen to *set* in
  the sea at:...Lord Howe Island

Distance from the lowest point
  (Lake Eyre, SA, 16 m below sea level)
  on the surface of Australia to the highest
  (Mount Kosciuszko, NSW, 2228 m):....................2244 m vertically;
                                   1358 km 'as cocky flies'

Distance from northernmost place
  on mainland Australia (Cape York,
  Queensland) to southernmost (South
  East Cape, Wilsons Promontory, Victoria):........................3184 km

Distance from Cape York to the
  southernmost point on the Tasmanian
  mainland (also South East Cape): ....3685 km

Distance from westernmost point
  (Steep Point, WA, near Carnarvon) on the
  mainland to easternmost (Cape Byron, NSW): .... 3894 km

Westernmost settlement in Australia: ....Useless Loop, WA,
                                     just inland from Steep Point

Easternmost settlement in Australia:...........Lord Howe Island, NSW

Northernmost settlement in Australia: ....Boigu Island, Qld

Southernmost settlement in Australia:...................Cockle Creek, Tas

Maximum draught for ships going
  through Torres Strait: ....12.2 m

HOLDEN MODELS

48–215/FX	1948–1953	VH	1981–1984
FJ	1953–1956	VK	1984–1986
FE	1956–1958	VL	1986–1988
FC	1958–1960	VN	1988–1991
FB	1960–1961	VP	1991–1992
EK	1961–1962	VP II	1992–1993
EJ	1962–1963	VR	1993–1994
EH	1963–1965	VR II	1994–1995
HD	1965–1966	VS	1995–1996
HR	1966–1968	VS II	1996–1997
HK	1968–1969	VT	1997–1999
HT	1969–1970	VS III	1998–2000
HG	1970–1971	VT II	1999–2000
HQ	1971–1974	VX	2000–2001
HJ	1974–1976	VX II	2001–2002
HX	1976–1977	VY	2002–2003
HZ	1977–1980	VY II	2003–2004
VB	1978–1980	VZ	2004–
VC	1980–1981		

MARRIAGE, 1885 STYLE

Married now one year ago,
Keeping house on Baxter Row,
Red-hot stove, beef-steak frying,
Girl got married, Cooking trying.
Cheeks all burning, eyes look red,
Girl got married, nearly dead,
Biscuits burned up, beef-steak chary,
Girl got married, awful sorry.

Palings 1885 Christmas Annual

BATHURST 500/1000 WINNERS

Held on the first Sunday in October over the Labour Day long weekend, the Bathurst 1000 is Australia's premier touring car race. Originally held at Phillip Island, Victoria, the race moved to the Mount Panorama Circuit at Bathurst, NSW, in 1963. It was changed from a 500-mile to a 1000-kilometre race in 1973. There were two 1000-kilometre events at Bathurst in both 1997 and 1998: the *AMP 1000* for 2-litre cars and the *Primus 1000 Classic* (1997) and the *FAI Bathurst 1000* (1998) for V8 Supercars. Since 1999 the race has been exclusively for V8 Supercars.

Year	Drivers	Car
Armstrong 500		
1960	John Roxburgh/Frank Coad	Vauxhall Cresta
1961	Bob Jane/Harry Firth	Mercedes 220SE
1962	Bob Jane/Harry Firth	XL Falcon
1963	Bob Jane/Harry Firth	Cortina GT
1964	Bob Jane/George Reynolds	Cortina GT
1965	Barry Seton/Midge Bosworth	Cortina GT500
Gallagher 500		
1966	Bob Holden/Rauno Aaltonen	Morris Cooper S
1967	Harry Firth/Fred Gibson	XR Falcon GT
Hardie Ferodo 500		
1968	Bruce McPhee/Barry Mulholland	Monaro GTS327
1969	Colin Bond/Tony Roberts	Monaro GTS350
1970	Allan Moffat	XW Falcon GTHO
1971	Allan Moffat	XY Falcon GTHO
1972	Peter Brock	Torana XU-1
Hardie Ferodo 1000		
1973	Allan Moffat/Ian Geoghegan	XA Falcon GT
1974	John Goss/Kevin Bartlett	XB Falcon GT
1975	Peter Brock/Brian Sampson	Torana L34
1976	Bob Morris/John Fitzpatrick	Torana L34
1977	Allan Moffat/Jackie Ickx	XC Falcon
1978	Peter Brock/Jim Richards	Torana A9X
1979	Peter Brock/Jim Richards	Torana A9X
1980	Peter Brock/Jim Richards	VC Commodore

Year	Drivers	Car

James Hardie 1000

1981	Dick Johnson/John French	XD Falcon
1982	Peter Brock/Larry Perkins	VH Commodore
1983	Peter Brock/Larry Perkins/John Harvey	VH Commodore
1984	Peter Brock/Larry Perkins	VK Commodore
1985	John Goss/Armin Hahne	Jaguar XJS
1986	Allan Grice/Graeme Bailey	VK Commodore
1987	Peter Brock/David Parsons/ Peter McLeod	VL Commodore

Tooheys 1000

1988	Tony Longhurst/Tomas Mezera	Sierra RS500
1989	Dick Johnson/John Bowe	Sierra RS500
1990	Allan Grice/Win Percy	VL Commodore
1991	Jim Richards/Mark Skaife	Nissan GT-R
1992	Jim Richards/Mark Skaife	Nissan GT-R
1993	Larry Perkins/Gregg Hansford	VP Commodore
1994	Dick Johnson/John Bowe	EB Falcon
1995	Larry Perkins/Russell Ingall	VR Commodore

AMP Bathurst 1000

1996	Craig Lowndes/Greg Murphy	VR Commodore
1997	Geoff Brabham/David Brabham	BMW 320i*
1998	Rickard Rydell/Jim Richards	Volvo S40*

Primus 1000 Classic

1997	Larry Perkins/Russell Ingall	Holden Commodore VS

FAI Bathurst 1000

1998	Jason Bright/Steven Richards	Ford Falcon EL
1999	Steven Richards/Greg Murphy	Holden Commodore VT
2000	Garth Tander/Jason Bargwanna	Holden Commodore VT

V8 Supercar Bathurst 1000

2001	Mark Skaife/Tony Longhurst	Holden Commodore VX

Bob Jane T-Marts 1000

2002	Mark Skaife/Jim Richards	Holden Commodore VX
2003	Greg Murphy/Rick Kelly	Holden Commodore VY
2004	Greg Murphy/Rick Kelly	Holden Commodore VY

* 2-litre Super Touring event

STATE CRICKET TEAMS

State	Sponsor	Team name
Western Australia	Retravision	Warriors
Victoria	Carlton Midstrength*	Bushrangers
South Australia	West End*	Redbacks
Tasmania	Cascade*	Tigers
New South Wales	Speed Blitz (Roads and Traffic Authority of NSW)	Blues
Queensland	XXXX Gold*	Bulls

* All beer brands

ORIGIN OF 'WOWSER'

I invented the word myself. I was the first man publicly to use the word. I first gave it public utterance in the City Council, when I applied it to Alderman Waterhouse, whom I referred to as the 'white, woolly, weary, watery, word-wasting wowser from Waverley'.

John Norton
editor of Sydney *Truth* and former Alderman, Sydney City

AUSTRALIA'S SHORTEST POEM?

REFLECTION ON MELBOURNE
Written in a Mood of Reverent Awe Occasioned by Reading the Works of Mr Ogden Nash

Wotta lotta
Terra Cotta!

D. Randolph Ayre
In *Lines*, annual journal of the Architectural Students' Society of the Royal Victorian Institute of Architects, 1938.

NATIONAL TEAM NICKNAMES

Hockey, Men's	*Kookaburras*
Hockey, Women's	*Hockeyroos*
Netball	—
Basketball, Men's	*Boomers*
Basketball, Women's	*Opals*
Rugby League	*Kangaroos*
Rugby Union	*Wallabies*
Soccer, Men's	*Socceroos*
Soccer, Women's	*Matildas*
Soccer, Olympic Men's	*Olyroos*
Water Polo, Men's	*Sharks*
Water Polo, Women's	—

CARNA PIES!

FOOTBALL TEAMS CALLED 'MAGPIES'

Team	Competition
Belconnen	ACTAFL
Bellingen	NSWCRL (Group 2)
Byron Bay	Summerland AFL
Collingwood	AFL
Claremont	SFL (Tasmania)
Devonport	Northern Tasmania FL
Glen Innes	NSWCRL (Group 19 – NERFL)
Maitland	NNSWSF
Mackay	Football [soccer] Queensland
Molong	NSWCRU (Central West)
Palmerston	Northern Territory FL
Port Adelaide	SANFL
Souths	QRU (BCR)
Souths Logan	QRL
Tamworth	NSWCRU (Central North)
Wagga	NSWCRL (Group 9)
Western Suburbs	NSWRL
Western Suburbs	Sydney AFL
Yass	CDRL
Yuendumu	CAFL

TRIBUTE BANDS, PAST AND PRESENT

Band	Tribute to
Abbacadabra	*ABBA*
ABBAlanche	*ABBA*
ACCA/DACCA	*AC/DC*
Alyce Platt – In The Flesh	*Blondie, The Motels, The Pretenders, Lena Lovitch, The Go-Gos, The Eurythmics, Katrina and the Waves*
Appetite for Destruction	*Guns 'n' Roses*
Atlantic Crossing	*Rod Stewart*
Atomic	*Blondie*
Australian U2 Show	*U2*
Babba	*ABBA*
Beatels	*The Beatles*
Beatnix	*The Beatles*
Believe	*Cher*
Beyond the Darkside	*Pink Floyd*
Big & Horny	*Joe Cocker, Blood Sweat and Tears, Chicago*
Bjorn Again	*ABBA*
Branded	*Rose Tattoo*
Buddy Holly Tribute Show	*Buddy Holly and the Crickets*
Cool Change	*Little River Band*
Creedence Clearwater Recycled	*Creedence Clearwater Revival*
Dancing Queen	*ABBA*
Dark Room	*The Angels*
Dean's Martini	*Dean Martin*
Dirty Deeds	*AC/DC*
Disstroyer	*KISS*
Elton Jack	*Elton John*
Face to Face	*The Angels*
Fat Bottomed Girls	*Queen*
Flogging a Dead Horse	*The Sex Pistols*
Fresh Cream	*Cream*
Gold Chisel	*Cold Chisel*

Band	Tribute to
Guru Hoodoos	*Hoodoo Gurus*
Heatwave	*Motown artists*
High Voltage	*AC/DC*
Inhalen	*Van Halen*
InVogue	*Madonna*
Inxsive	*INXS*
Joshua Tree	*U2*
KISSTERIA	*KISS*
KISStroyer	*KISS*
Led Zepped	*Led Zeppelin*
Let It Be Beatles	*The Beatles*
Little Lies	*Fleetwood Mac*
Live Wire	*Mötley Crüe*
Live Wire	*Bon Scott*
Meat Balls	*Meat Loaf*
Mikey Spunk and his Glitter Balls	*KISS, AC/DC, Marc Bolan, Rolling Stones, ABBA, Duran Duran, Slade, Noosha Fox, Sweet, Skyhooks, Bay City Rollers*
Mo-Tunes	*Motown artists*
Neely Diamond	*Neil Diamond*
New Jersey	*Bon Jovi*
No Secrets	*The Angels*
Oh Boy	*Buddy Holly and the Crickets*
100% Kylie	*Kylie Minogue*
Phil Haley and His Comments	*Bill Haley and His Comets*
Queen Essential	*Queen*
Quill	*Mötley Crüe, Poison, Ratt, Saxon, Whitesnake, Ozzy Osbourne*
Quo Vadis	*Status Quo*
Rattle and Hum	*U2*
Really Joel	*Billy Joel*
Re-mones	*The Ramones*

Band	Tribute to
Ricky Loca	*Ricky Martin*
Ricky Martin Tribute Show	*Ricky Martin*
Seattle Jam	*Pearl Jam*
Seattle Sound	*Nirvana, Pearl Jam, Soundgarden, Stone Temple Pilots, Alice in Chains*
Sexed Up	*Robbie Williams*
Shake a Tailfeather	*The Blues Brothers*
South of the Abyss	*Slayer*
Stand and Deliver	*Adam and the Ants, Duran Duran, Madonna*
Stayin' Alive	*The Bee Gees*
The Australian Status Quo Show	*Status Quo*
The Beach Balls	*The Beach Boys*
The Big O Show	*Roy Orbison*
The Dave Graney Show	*Dave Graney and the Coral Snakes**
The Ego Has Landed	*Robbie Williams*
The Elton Experience	*Elton John*
The Fab Four	*The Beatles*
The Joe Cocker and Tina Turner Tribute Show	*Joe Cocker, Tina Turner*
The Living Years	*Mike and the Mechanics*
The Pepper Heads	*Red Hot Chili Peppers*
The Real Thing	*U2*
The Robbee Williams Show	*Robbie Williams*
The Slayer Show	*Slayer*
The Stones – A Musical Tribute	*The Rolling Stones*
The SuperTRONICS	*The Shadows, Dick Dale, The Ventures*
The Voice	*John Farnham*
Thunderstuck	*AC/DC*
Twin Lizzy	*Thin Lizzy*
Van Hagar	*Van Halen, David Lee Roth, Sammy Hagar*

Band	Tribute to
War Pigs	*Black Sabbath, Ozzy Osbourne*
We Are The Champions	*Queen*
Where's Ringo	*The Beatles*
YMCA	*The Village People*
Zeppelin Live	*Led Zeppelin*
Zero	*Smashing Pumpkins*

* 'The Dave Graney Show' was actually fronted by Dave Graney himself.

SOME SHIPWRECKS

Batavia

On a trip from Holland to Java in 1628, the *Batavia* ran aground on a reef near the Houtman Abrolhos Islands, 50 km off present-day Geraldton, WA. The commander, Francis Pelsaert, took one rowboat and eventually reached Java, returning with the frigate *Sardam* to rescue the castaways. On the islands a crewman, Jeronimus Cornelisz, began a mutiny. The mutineers killed all they thought might oppose them, with the toll eventually reaching 125. Only about 40 soldiers resisted Cornelisz by retreating to another island. When Pelsaert returned, eight men, including Cornelisz, were hanged. Two men being taken back to Java for trial pleaded with Pelsaert to be set down on the coast of WA. They were never seen again.

Stirling Castle

Wrecked in a storm off southern Queensland in 1836. In two rowboats, the 17 surviving passengers and crew attempted to reach Moreton Bay (now Brisbane), but on Great Sandy Island (now Fraser Island) they were taken captive by Aborigines and forced into slavery. The most famous survivor of the wreck, Eliza Fraser, became a slave to a group of women. Eventually John Graham, a convict at Moreton Bay who had earlier escaped and lived in the bush with the Aborigines before giving himself up, heard from Aboriginal friends that there were 'ghosts' living with the tribes on Great Sandy Island. Graham then accompanied a party from Moreton Bay which located the survivors, including Mrs Fraser.

Dunbar

Ran aground on North Head, Sydney Harbour in 1857, with the loss of 121 people. The only survivor was a sailor, James Johnson.

Cawarra

Paddlewheel steamer trying to escape a storm by entering Newcastle Harbour in 1866. Waves crashing over her reached the engine room and put out the fires of the engines. The *Cawarra* soon sank, with the only survivor of 25 passengers and 35 crew being a sailor, Frederick Hedges. He was rescued by none other than James Johnson, the only survivor of the *Dunbar*, who was working at Newcastle's lighthouse.

Loch Ard

Clipper ship which left London in 1878 with 36 crew and 17 passengers. Nearly half the passengers were the Carmichael family, emigrating from Ireland. The captain missed seeing the Cape Otway light and sailed dangerously close to shore and hit a reef off Mutton Bird Island. The only survivors were a sailor, Tom Pearce, and Eva Carmichael, both around the same age, who survived by being washed into what is now Loch Ard Gorge.

Greycliffe

On 3 November 1927, the Union Steamship Company's mail steamer *Tahiti* cut the Sydney Harbour ferry *Greycliffe* in two, resulting in the death of 40 passengers. The tragedy was made worse by the fact that most of the dead came from one part of Sydney, Watsons Bay, to which the *Greycliffe* had been travelling from Circular Quay. The pilot of the *Tahiti*, Thomas Carson, lived in Watsons Bay, surrounded by many of the victims' families, and his family became *persona non grata* for some members of the community. The accident later found its way into fiction: a version of it appears in Sumner Locke Elliott's novel *Careful, He Might Hear You*.

Kuttabul

Sydney Harbour ferry being used as a floating dormitory at Garden Island in Sydney Harbour in 1942. Three Japanese two-man midget submarines infiltrated Sydney Harbour and fired a torpedo which narrowly missed the cruiser USS *Chicago*, and another which passed under a Dutch submarine and exploded beneath the *Kuttabul*. Nineteen naval ratings were killed. Of the Japanese submarines, one blew itself up after being caught in the anti-torpedo net stretched across the harbour, another was destroyed by depth charges, while the third escaped but never reached its mother ship.

HMAS *Sydney*

Following a battle with the German raider HSK *Kormoran* off the Western Australian coast, the light cruiser HMAS *Sydney* disappeared almost without trace on 19 November 1941. The *Kormoran* also sank. The loss of the *Sydney* with its full complement of 645 is Australia's worst naval disaster and one of its greatest wartime mysteries. The only confirmed relics found were a lifebelt and a Carley life float damaged by shellfire. Of the *Kormoran*'s crew of 397, there were 317 survivors.

Centaur

The unarmed and brightly lit hospital ship *Centaur* was east of Moreton Island, off the Queensland coast, when it was torpedoed at 4.10 am on 14 May 1943 by Japanese Submarine 1–177 commanded by Lieutenant-Commander Nakagawa. The attack seems to have been Nakagawa's decision as commander and not the result of official policy. Out of a complement of 332, only 64 from the *Centaur* survived: the highest death toll of any merchant vessel sunk by submarine in the Pacific during World War II. The Australian Army's 2/12 Field Ambulance, which was on its way to Port Moresby, was virtually wiped out. Of 12 nurses, only Sister Ellen Savage survived.

AUSTRALIAN WINE REGIONS

NSW and ACT

Zones	Regions	Varieties grown
Big Rivers Zone	Murray Darling (NSW & Vic)	Chardonnay, Cabernet Sauvignon, Muscat Gordo Blanco, Semillon, Colombard
	Perricoota	Chardonnay, Cabernet Sauvignon, Merlot, Shiraz
	Riverina	Chardonnay, Chenin Blanc, Gewürztraminer, Marsanne, Semillon, Verdelho, Cabernet Sauvignon, Merlot, Pinot Noir, Shiraz
	Swan Hill (NSW & Vic)	Cabernet, Shiraz, Chardonnay, Riesling, Durif, Sangiovese
Central Ranges	Cowra	Chardonnay, Cabernet Sauvignon, Merlot, Shiraz, Gewürztraminer, Sauvignon Blanc, Riesling
	Mudgee (Nest in the Hills)	Shiraz, Cabernet Sauvignon, Chardonnay
	Orange	Cabernet, Chardonnay
Hunter Valley	Hunter (Lower and Upper)	Semillon, Shiraz, Cabernet Sauvignon, Merlot, Pinot Noir, Chardonnay, Riesling, Sauvignon Blanc
	Sub-region Broke Fordwich	Chardonnay, Semillon, Traminer, Verdelho, Cabernet Sauvignon, Merlot, Shiraz

Zones	Regions	Varieties grown
Northern Rivers	Hastings River	Chambourcin, Cabernet Franc, Cabernet Sauvignon, Merlot, Shiraz, Chardonnay, Sauvignon Blanc, Semillon
Northern Slopes	—	
South Coast	Shoalhaven Coast	Chambourcin, Chardonnay, Gewürztraminer, Sauvignon Blanc, Semillon, Verdelho, Cabernet Sauvignon, Merlot, Shiraz
	Southern Highlands	Chardonnay, Riesling, Sauvignon Blanc, Cabernet Sauvignon, Pinot Noir, Shiraz
Southern NSW	Canberra District	Chardonnay, Riesling
	Gundagai	Semillon, Chardonnay, Sauvignon Blanc, Cabernet Sauvignon, Merlot, Shiraz
	Hilltops	Cabernet Sauvignon, Merlot, Pinot Noir, Chardonnay, Riesling, Sauvignon Blanc, Semillon, Zinfandel
	Tumbarumba	Chardonnay, Sauvignon Blanc, Pinot Noir
Western Plains	—	

Northern Territory
The Northern Territory has no regions or sub-regions.

Queensland

Zones	Regions	Varieties grown
Queensland	Granite Belt	Shiraz, Cabernet Sauvignon, Chardonnay, Sauvignon Blanc, Semillon
	South Burnett	Chardonnay, Riesling, Sauvignon Blanc, Semillon, Cabernet Sauvignon, Merlot, Shiraz

South Australia

Adelaide Superzone includes Barossa, Fleurieu and Mount Lofty Ranges zones.

Zones	Regions	Varieties grown
Barossa	Barossa Valley	Shiraz, Cabernet Sauvignon, Riesling, Chardonnay, Semillon, Grenache
	Eden Valley	Riesling, Chardonnay, Shiraz
	Sub-region High Eden	Riesling, Chardonnay, Cabernet Sauvignon, Shiraz
Far North	Southern Flinders Ranges	Cabernet Sauvignon, Merlot, Shiraz
Fleurieu	Currency Creek	Chardonnay, Sauvignon Blanc, Cabernet Sauvignon, Shiraz
	Kangaroo Island	Chardonnay, Cabernet Franc, Cabernet Sauvignon, Merlot, Shiraz
	Langhorne Creek	Chardonnay, Verdelho, Cabernet Sauvignon (including Shalistin and Malian), Merlot, Shiraz

Zones	Regions	Varieties grown
	McLaren Vale	Cabernet Sauvignon, Shiraz, Malbec, Merlot, Chardonnay, Semillon, Grenache, Sauvignon Blanc, Riesling, Verdelho
	Southern Fleurieu	Riesling, Viognier, Cabernet Sauvignon, Malbec, Shiraz
Limestone Coast	Coonawarra	Cabernet Sauvignon. Shiraz, Petit Verdot, Pinot Noir, Malbec, Merlot, Sauvignon Blanc, Chardonnay, Riesling, Semillon
	Mount Benson	Chardonnay, Sauvignon Blanc, Cabernet Sauvignon, Shiraz, Merlot, Viognier
	Padthaway	Chardonnay, Cabernet Sauvignon, Shiraz
	Penola	Cabernet Sauvignon, Shiraz
	Wrattonbully	Cabernet Sauvignon, Shiraz
Lower Murray	Riverland	Muscat Gordo Blanc, Grenache, Chardonnay, Cabernet Sauvignon, Shiraz
Mounty Lofty Ranges	Adelaide Hills	Chardonnay, Pinot Noir, Riesling, Sauvignon Blanc, Semillon, Cabernet Sauvignon, Merlot, Sangiovese, Shiraz
	Sub-regions	
	Lenswood	Chardonnay, Pinot Noir
	Piccadilly Valley	Chardonnay, Pinot Noir

Zones	Regions	Varieties grown
	Adelaide Plains	Chardonnay, Shiraz, Cabernet Sauvignon, Grenache, Sauvignon Blanc, Riesling, Semillon
	Clare Valley	Cabernet Sauvignon, Shiraz, Riesling, Chardonnay

Peninsulas Zone, The — —

Tasmania

Tasmania is one zone with no regions.

Northen Tasmania: Chardonnay, Riesling, Sauvignon Blanc, Pinot Noir, Cabernet Sauvignon, Merlot

Southern Tasmania: Pinot Noir, Chardonnay, Gewürztraminer, Riesling, Sauvignon Blanc

Victoria

Zones	Regions	Varieties grown
Central Victoria	Bendigo	Cabernet Sauvignon, Shiraz, Chardonnay, Sauvignon Blanc, Viognier
	Goulburn Valley	Shiraz, Cabernet Sauvignon, Marsanne
	Sub-region Nagambie Lakes	Marsanne, Roussanne, Viognier, Grenache, Shiraz, Mourvèdre (Mataro), Riesling, Verdelho, Chardonnay, Merlot, Cabernet Sauvignon
	Heathcote	Shiraz, Cabernet Sauvignon

Zones	Regions	Varieties grown
	Strathbogie Ranges	Chardonnay, Riesling, Pinot Gris, Sauvignon Blanc, Cabernet Sauvignon, Cabernet Franc, Pinot Noir, Merlot
	Upper Goulburn	Chardonnay, Gewürztraminer, Pinot Noir, Sauvignon Blanc, Riesling, Cabernet Sauvignon, Merlot, Shiraz
Gippsland	No official regions	Chardonnay, Pinot Noir
North East Victoria	Alpine Valleys	Chardonnay, Sauvignon Blanc, Cabernet Sauvignon, Merlot, Pinot Noir, Shiraz
	Beechworth	Pinot Noir, Riesling, Chardonnay
	Glenrowan	Shiraz, Chardonnay
	King Valley	Chardonnay, Cabernet Sauvignon
	Rutherglen	Muscat, Tokay
North West Victoria	Murray Darling (Vic & NSW)	Chardonnay, Cabernet Sauvignon, Muscat Gordo Blanco, Semillon, Colombard
	Swan Hill (Vic & NSW)	Cabernet, Shiraz, Chardonnay, Riesling, Durif, Sangiovese
Port Phillip	Geelong	Chardonnay, Pinot Gris, Riesling, Sauvignon Blanc, Semillon Cabernet Sauvignon, Malbec, Merlot, Pinot Noir, Shiraz

Zones	Regions	Varieties grown
	Macedon Ranges	Chardonnay, Riesling, Sauvignon Blanc, Semillon, Traminer, Cabernet Franc, Cabernet Sauvignon, Merlot, Pinot Noir, Shiraz
	Mornington Peninsula	Chardonnay, Pinot Noir, Shiraz, Cabernet Sauvignon, Malbec, Merlot, Pinot Gris, Riesling
	Sunbury	Chardonnay, Sauvignon Blanc, Semillon, Cabernet Sauvignon, Pinot Noir, Shiraz
	Yarra Valley	Cabernet Sauvignon, Cabernet Franc, Merlot, Pinot Noir, Shiraz, Chardonnay, Gewürztraminer, Semillon, Marsanne, Riesling, Verduzzo
Western Victoria	Grampians	Chardonnay, Riesling, Cabernet Sauvignon, Shiraz, Ondenc, Chasselas
	Henty	Chardonnay, Riesling, Meunier, Pinot Noir, Shiraz
	Pyrenees	Shiraz, Cabernet Sauvignon

Western Australia

Zones	Regions	Varieties grown
Central Western Australia	— —	
Eastern Plains, Inland & North of WA	— —	
Greater Perth	Peel	Chardonnay, Chenin Blanc, Semillon, Verdelho, Cabernet Sauvignon, Merlot, Shiraz
	Perth Hills	Chardonnay, Chenin Blanc, Cabernet Sauvignon, Shiraz, Pinot Noir
	Swan District	Chenin Blanc, Verdelho
	Sub-region Swan Valley	Chardonnay, Chenin Blanc, Semillon, Verdelho, Cabernet Sauvignon, Merlot, Shiraz, Muscat Gordo Blanco, Muscadelle
South West Australia	Blackwood Valley	Chardonnay, Riesling, Sauvignon Blanc, Semillon, Cabernet Sauvignon, Shiraz
	Geographe	Chardonnay, Sauvignon Blanc, Cabernet Sauvignon, Merlot, Pinot Noir, Shiraz
	Great Southern *Sub-regions*	
	Albany	Pinot Noir, Chardonnay
	Denmark	Chardonnay, Pinot Noir, Cabernet Franc, Cabernet Sauvignon Shiraz, Sauvignon Blanc, Semillon

Zones	Regions	Varieties grown
	Frankland River	Chardonnay, Riesling, Sauvignon Blanc, Cabernet Sauvignon, Shiraz
	Mount Barker	Riesling, Pinot Noir, Shiraz, Chardonnay, Cabernet Sauvignon, Cabernet Franc, Sauvignon Blanc, Semillon, Malbec, Merlot
	Porongurup	Chardonnay, Riesling, Semillon, Verdelho, Cabernet Franc, Cabernet Sauvignon, Pinot Noir, Merlot, Shiraz
	Manjimup	Chardonnay, Sauvignon Blanc, Verdelho, Cabernet Sauvignon, Pinot Noir
	Margaret River	Chardonnay, Cabernet Sauvignon, Shiraz
	Pemberton (Karri Country)	Chardonnay, Sauvignon Blanc, Semillon, Verdelho, Cabernet Sauvignon, Merlot, Pinot Noir, Shiraz
West Australian South East Coastal	—	

Source: Australian Wine and Brandy Corporation

THE STANDARD GLASS OF WINE

A standard drink is 10 g of alcohol, which equals 100 mL of wine. To stay below the legal blood alcohol level of 0.05, men should drink no more than 2 standard drinks in the first hour followed by 1 standard drink per hour, and for women, no more than 1 standard drink per hour.

AUSTRALIA'S MOST NOTORIOUS
GHOSTS AND HAUNTINGS

Casey's Ghost	*Duntroon, ACT*
Fisher's Ghost	*Campbelltown, NSW*
Isle of the Dead	*Port Arthur, Tas*
Luna Park Joker Ghost	*St Kilda, Vic*
Mater Hospital	*Crows Nest, NSW*
Min Min Light	*Boulia, Qld*
Monte Cristo Homestead	*Junee, NSW*
North Head Quarantine Station	*Manly, NSW*
Picton Tunnel	*Picton, NSW*
Theatre Royal	*Hobart, Tas*

FIVE FAST FOOD FIRSTS

First KFC	Guildford, NSW	1968
First Pizza Hut	Belfield, NSW	1970
First McDonald's	Yagoona, NSW	1971
First Starbucks	Sydney, NSW	2000
First Krispy Kreme	Penrith, NSW	2003

THE RIGHTS OF WOMEN

According to a member of the Western Australian Parliament in 1898, during a debate on the woman suffrage issue:

The rights of women what are they?
The right to labour and to pray
The right to watch while others sleep;
The right o'er others' woes to weep.

HUNTER VALLEY PLACE NAMES

Place	Origin of name
Cardiff	*Wales*
Hexham	*Northumberland, England*
Jesmond	*Tyneside, England*
Mayfield	*Northumberland, England*
Morpeth	*Northumberland, England*
Newcastle	*Tyneside, England*
Stanford Merthyr	*Wales*
Stockton	*Teesside, England*
Swansea	*Wales*
Wallsend	*Tyneside, England*

A BRIEF GUIDE TO AUSTRALIAN CULTURE

Australian universities give the following briefs on Australian culture for their foreign prospective students:

University of Queensland
'Australians like to abbreviate or shorten words, even down to initial letters. So food technology is usually shortened to "food tech", "breakfast" becomes "brekkie", and a tutorial becomes a "tute".'

'Young people may enter into sexual relationships without any future planning or thoughts about marriage. Parents may not like those situations but living together before marriage is very common. Sometimes two women or men are living together in a gay or lesbian relationship.'

'At the end of the evening, your date may invite you into his/her place for a drink. It is possible that the invitation may or may not suggest more than just coffee. You are the best judge as to whether to accept or to decline the invitation.'

'If you are used to having servants to do most of your work, you may find the Australian way of life a little difficult at first. In Australia, it is not considered shameful for anyone to do manual work and males often share in the housework.'

'Australians eat with their fingers only at barbecues or picnics outside the home.'

'Most Australians want to be treated as individuals rather than as representatives of a certain class, position or group. They dislike being too dependent on others.'

University of Sydney
'Always swim between the flags when you are at the beach. Do not dive into the water if you do not know how deep it is. When in the sun always use a factor 15+ sun screen as the Australian sun is very harsh and skin cancer rates are high.'

'Prices are "fixed" in Australia even in Paddy's Market and other markets. Bargaining is not expected.'

'To avoid your drinks being spiked, ALWAYS buy your own and NEVER leave it unattended.'

'On occasions, the [Campus] Security Service may be called to attend . . . functions because someone is threatening to harm themselves or others. They are not there to hinder your enjoyment in any way but to ensure that all activities are conducted in a safe and sensible manner.'

University of NSW
'Partly because of the diverse cultural background of its people, Australians are generally relatively accommodating and tolerant of other cultures and sensitive to differing religious beliefs. You will also find that there is a large variety of different accents which exist in Australian society.'

'While in Australia you will have no trouble finding an appropriate place of worship.'

University of Melbourne
'Australians often communicate with a form of humour and gentle irony, usually used to express friendliness and break the ice; hence it should not to be taken too seriously.'

'In Australia, it really pays to be polite and courteous when interacting in society. The "excuse me", "good morning/afternoon/evening", "please" and "thank you"s will generally give you a much better response and service than the typical same setting in Asia. It really makes a big difference.' – Benjamin Tan, Singapore

Macquarie University
'As you settle and make friends, you will find that there is really no such thing as a "typical" Australian.'

'Nicknames are a sign of acceptance and friendship.'

'Australians are known for their unique sense of humour. This often involves light-hearted teasing and is often termed by Australians as "taking the piss". Humour may also be centred on people who are different, with different accents, clothes and habits. In most cases you should not take offence.'

'You should try to be as punctual as possible. Even though it might seem like everyone is very easy-going, Australians do not like to wait or have their time wasted.'

Monash University
'Australia is renowned for:
• Friendly and open-minded people
• A cultural bridge between East and West
• An academic tradition of intellectual inquiry
• A healthy outdoor lifestyle

- Pleasant climate
- State-of-the-art communication systems
- Safe and efficient transport
- A fair and stable democracy'

University of Adelaide
'Some newcomers say that Australians speak with their lips tightly shut.'

'A word for the wise though – just because we natives might throw in a "bloody oath mate!" Or the occasional "Crikey! A dingo ate me baby!" doesn't mean that you can. It's kind of like being a part of a club. If you can't do the accent perfectly, then you're not a member, so don't even try . . . If we call you an idiot or a spastic wanker, it means we like you and consider you a friend.'

University of Wollongong
'Australians do not stand very close to others or touch them much during conversation. It is not an insult in Australia if you are handed something with the left hand.'

REFERENDUM RESULTS

Year	Question	Result
1906	Enabling holding Senate elections concurrently with House of Representatives	*Carried*
1910	(i) Giving Commonwealth power to take over State debts	*Carried*
	(ii) Fixed payment by Commonwealth to States out of surplus revenue on per capita basis	*Not carried*
1911	(i) Extending Commonwealth powers over trade and commerce, the control of corporations, labour and employment, including wages and conditions and the settling of disputes, and combinations and monopolies	*Not carried*
	(ii) Giving Commonwealth power to nationalise monopolies in industries	*Not carried*
1913	(i) Extending Commonwealth powers over trade and commerce	*Not carried*
	(ii) Extending Commonwealth powers over the control of corporations	*Not carried*
	(iii) Extending Commonwealth powers over industrial matters	*Not carried*
	(iv) Extending Commonwealth powers over trusts (i.e. combinations and monopolies)	*Not carried*
	(v) Giving Commonwealth power to nationalise monopolies in industries	*Not carried*
	(vi) Extending Commonwealth powers over railways disputes	*Not carried*
1916	Gauging support for military conscription	*Not carried*
1917	Gauging support for military conscription	*Not carried*
1919	(i) Temporarily extending Commonwealth powers over trade and commerce, corporations, industrial matters and trusts	*Not carried*
	(ii) Temporarily giving Commonwealth power to nationalise monopolies in industries	*Not carried*

Year	Question	Result
1926	(i) Extending Commonwealth powers over industrial relations and commerce	*Not carried*
	(ii) Empowering Commonwealth to take measures to protect the public against interruption of essential services	*Not carried*
1928	Terminating per-capita payments from Commonwealth to States, and reforming system of State borrowing	*Carried*
1937	(i) Giving Commonwealth power to legislate with respect to air navigation and aircraft	*Not carried*
	(ii) Giving Commonwealth power to legislate with respect to marketing	*Not carried*
1944	Giving Commonwealth power, for a period of five years, to legislate with respect to the 'Fourteen Points' relating to post-war reconstruction and guarantees of democratic rights	*Not carried*
1946	(i) Giving Commonwealth power to legislate on a wide range of social services	*Carried*
	(ii) Giving Commonwealth power to legislate with respect to organised marketing of primary products	*Not carried*
	(iii) Giving Commonwealth power to legislate with respect to terms and conditions of industrial employment	*Not carried*
1948	Giving Commonwealth permanent power (previously a temporary wartime measure) to control rents and prices	*Not carried*
1951	Giving Commonwealth power to make laws in respect of Communists and Communism where this was necessary for the security of the Commonwealth	*Not carried*
1967	(i) Altering Constitution so that the number of Members of the House of Representatives	

Year	Question	Result
	could be increased without necessarily increasing the number of Senators	*Not carried*
	(ii) Seeking to remove any ground for the belief that the Constitution discriminated against Aboriginal people, and giving Commonwealth power to enact special laws for them	*Carried*
1973	(i) Giving power to Commonwealth to control prices	*Not carried*
	(ii) Giving power to Commonwealth to control incomes	*Not carried*
1974	(i) Ensuring elections for the Senate and the House of Representatives held on the same day	*Not carried*
	(ii) Giving a vote in referendums to electors in ACT and NT, and secondly to enable amendments to be made to the Constitution if approved by a majority of Australian voters and a majority of voters in half the States (previously in a majority of the States)	*Not carried*
	(iii) Making population (previously electors) the basis of determining the average size of electorates in each State	*Not carried*
	(iv) Giving Commonwealth powers to borrow money for, and to make financial assistance grants directly to, any local government body	*Not carried*
1977	(i) Ensuring elections for the Senate and the House of Representatives held on the same day	*Not carried*
	(ii) Ensuring as far as practicable that a casual vacancy in the Senate is filled by a person of the same political party as the Senator chosen by the people and that that person shall hold the seat for the balance of the term	*Carried*
	(iii) Allowing electors in Territories to vote at referendums on proposed laws to alter the Constitution	*Carried*

Year	Question	Result
	(iv) Providing for retiring ages for judges of Federal Courts	*Carried*
1984	(i) Ensuring elections for the Senate and the House of Representatives held on the same day	*Not carried*
	(ii) Enabling Commonwealth and States to voluntarily refer powers to each other	*Not carried*
1988	(i) Providing for four-year maximum terms for members of both Houses of the Commonwealth Parliament	*Not carried*
	(ii) Seeking to ensure fair and democratic parliamentary elections throughout Australia	*Not carried*
	(iii) Seeking to recognise local government	*Not carried*
	(iv) Seeking to extend the right to trial by jury, to extend freedom of religion, and to ensure fair terms for persons whose property is acquired by any Government	*Not carried*
1999	(i) Establishing the Commonwealth of Australia as a republic with the Queen and Governor-General being replaced by a President appointed by a two-thirds majority of the members of the Commonwealth Parliament	*Not carried*
	(ii) Altering the Constitution to insert a preamble	*Not carried*

Carried: 8
Not carried: 38

MALCOLM TURNBULL, CHAIRMAN OF THE AUSTRALIAN REPUBLICAN MOVEMENT, ON THE 1999 REPUBLIC REFERENDUM RESULT

'To those republicans who voted No thinking they will soon get another chance to vote [on a different model], I am afraid you have been had.'

CONSPIRACY THEORIES

Harold Holt

The disappearance of Australia's prime minister while swimming off Cheviot Beach was one of the most unusual deaths of a national leader ever, although it was a very Australian one. The unlikelihood of a prime minister simply disappearing has led to claims that he was taken by a Chinese submarine: either that he was kidnapped, or he had been a Chinese spy and was now escaping. The response of his widow, Dame Zara: 'Harry? Chinese submarine? He didn't even like Chinese cooking.'

Sir John Kerr and the Whitlam Dismissal

Christopher Boyce, a clerk at TRW Defense and Space Systems with access to classified material, turned traitor when he found that the CIA was withholding intelligence information from Australia when Gough Whitlam was prime minister, and trying to infiltrate Australia's trade unions. The 1975 dismissal of Whitlam by Governor-General Sir John Kerr is referred to in the 1982 Midnight Oil song *The Power and the Passion*. 'Uncle Sam and John', go the lyrics, are 'quite enough' to get rid of Whitlam. The 1983 television miniseries *The Dismissal* also hints at CIA involvement in Australian internal politics, but takes the matter no further.

Martin Bryant

The toughening of gun-ownership laws in the wake of the Port Arthur Massacre of 1996 has led to claims that Martin Bryant could not have been the killer, and that the massacre was a conspiracy to disarm Australia. Ian Murphy, founder of the militia group Australian Freedom Scouts, said in 1999: 'It smells, the whole thing looks dreadful. And I mean it's important from everyone's point of view that the truth is told. This could be as big a matter as the assassination of President Kennedy.'

Migration
In his 1984 book *All for Australia*, the historian Geoffrey Blainey likened the process for selecting immigrants to a cricket scoreboard: seemingly open and non-racially-based, but actually with a secret room inside where the scores were rigged to favour Asian immigrants over Europeans. (While Blainey himself welcomed the end of the White Australia Policy, he was concerned about how successfully non-European immigrants were integrating into Australian society.) In a 1997 *Bulletin* poll, 41 per cent of respondents said information about the impact of immigration was being covered up; 40 per cent said the same thing was happening with respect to alien visitation.

STATE NICKNAMES

New South Welsh	*Cornstalks*
Victorians	*Cabbage patchers*
Queenslanders	*Bananabenders*
South Australians	*Croweaters*
Western Australians	*Sandgropers*
Tasmanians	*Apple islanders*

A TOP FIVE: WORST AUSSIE ACCENTS IN HOLLYWOOD FILMS

Actor	Film
Meryl Streep	*Evil Angels* aka *A Cry in the Dark*
James Coburn	*The Great Escape*
Kevin Kline	*Fierce Creatures*
James Mason	*Age of Consent*
Richard Harris	*The Guns of Navarone*

PSEUDONYMS IN CLIVE JAMES'
AUTOBIOGRAPHIES

Pseudonym	For
Bruce Jennings	*Barry Humphries*
Romaine Rand	*Germaine Greer*
Dave Dalziel	*Bruce Beresford*
Huggins	*Robert Hughes*
The Rajguptas or 'The Beautiful Indians'	*Sonny and Gita Mehta*
Dibbs Buckley	*Brett Whiteley*
Delish Buckley	*Wendy Whiteley*

TOURED AUSTRALIA, APRIL–MAY 1979

Tom Waits

Melbourne: Palais Theatre	Tuesday, May 1
Sydney: State Theatre	Wednesday, May 2
Canberra: Canberra Theatre	Friday, May 4
Brisbane: Festival Hall	Saturday, May 5
Adelaide: Festival Theatre	Tuesday, May 8
Perth: Concert Hall	Friday, May 11

Julian Bream

Adelaide: Festival Theatre	Thursday, April 26
Sydney: Opera House	Saturday, April 28
Sydney: Seymour Centre	Monday, April 30
Melbourne: Dallas Brooks Hall	Tuesday, May 1

Bob Marley and the Wailers

Brisbane: Festival Hall	Wednesday, April 18
Adelaide: Apollo Stadium	Friday, April 20
Perth: Entertainment Centre	Monday, April 23
Melbourne: Festival Hall	Wednesday, April 25
Sydney: Hordern Pavillion	Friday, April 27

ORANA REGION, NSW: TOURIST ATTRACTIONS

Western Plains Zoo, Dubbo
Warrumbungle National Park
Anglo-Australian Telescope, Siding Spring
Opal mines, Lightning Ridge

PORT AUGUSTA TO KALGOORLIE ON THE TRANS-CONTINENTAL RAILWAY

Port Augusta	Hughes
Hesso	
Pimba (Woomera)	*SA–WA border*
Kingoonya	Deakin
Tarcoola	Reid
Malbooma	Forrest
Wynbring	Loongana
Mt Christie	Nurina
Mungala	Haig
Barton	Rawlinna
Bates	Naretha
Ooldea	Kitchener
Watson	Zanthus
O'Malley	Chifley
Fisher	Karonie
Cook	Randell
Denman	Kalgoorlie

ORD RIVER SCHEME, WA – WHAT WENT WRONG

Cotton ....rising costs, ineffective pesticides, falling yields and quality
Rice ....destroyed by zinc deficiency
Peanuts ....erratic yields
Safflower ....poor quality
Wheat and sugar..non-viable

ATTENDED THE SAME SCHOOL

Abbotsleigh ....Georgie Parker, Meredith Burgmann
Aquinas ....Terry Alderman, Fred Chaney
Balgowlah Boys High ....Iain Murray, David Oldfield
Barker...Peter Garrett, Philip Ruddock
Brighton Grammar...............................Warwick Capper, Peter Reith
Brisbane State High...................................Wally Lewis, Hayley Lewis
Canberra Girls Grammar ....Kate Fisher, Patricia Hewitt
Canberra Grammar ....David Eastman (dux of school),
James O'Loghlin
Canterbury Boys High ....John Howard (the prime minister),
Max Suich
Carey Baptist Grammar ....John Elliott, Steve Vizard
Caulfield Grammar...............................Nick Cave, Christopher Skase
Christian Brothers, St Kilda................Eddie McGuire, Daryl Somers
Eltham High..Phillip Adams, Peter Brock
Epping Boys High ....Geoffrey Robertson, Jack Newton
Essendon Grammar.....................Jason and Mark Moran, Eric Bana
Fintona...Beryl Beaurepaire, Helen Caldicott
Fort Street High ....Michael Kirby, Deborah Hutton
Friends' ....Errol Flynn, Max Walker
Geelong Grammar....................................Peter Carey, Prince Charles
Guildford Grammar ....Heath Ledger, Arnold Potts
(21 Brigade commander, Kokoda Track, 1942)
Hale ....Richard Court, Clive Robertson
Homebush Boys High ....Neil Armfield, Roger Rogerson
Ipswich Grammar ..................................J.J.C. Bradfield, Harry Gibbs
Kincoppal-Rose Bay ....Nikki Gemmell, Princess Michael of Kent
Knox Grammar ....Gough Whitlam, John Howard (the actor)
Kogarah High ....Clive James, John Hewson
Launceston Grammar...........................David Boon, Indira Naidoo
Lauriston.......................................Felicity Kennett, Deborah Conway
Melbourne Grammar ....Barry Humphries, Manning Clark
Melbourne High ....Lindsay Fox, Athol Guy
Nambour State High...................................Kevin Rudd, Bernard King

North Sydney Boys High ......Alan Border, Greedy Smith (same year)
North Sydney Girls High ....Nicole Kidman, Margaret Throsby
Northcote High ....Jac Nasser, Normie Rowe
Parramatta High ....Richie Benaud, Chips Rafferty
Perth Modern ....Bob Hawke, John Stone
PLC, Melbourne...............Henry Handel Richardson, Nettie Palmer
Preston Tech ....Bill Lawry, Ron Barassi
Prince Alfred ....Ian, Greg and Trevor Chappell,
                                                                              Robert Helpmann
Ravenswood ....Gretel Killeen (school captain),
                                                                              Tammin Sursok
Riverview (St Ignatius)...........................Tony Abbott, Robert Hughes
Sacred Heart, Somerton Park ....Bart Cummings, Shaun Micallef
SCEGGS ....Claudia Karvan, Pamela Stephenson
Scotch College...Jeff Kennett, John Cain snr
St Aloysius......................Charles, Malcolm and Alistair Mackerras,
                                                                              Billy Birmingham
St Joseph's, Hunters Hill ....Robbie Waterhouse,
                                                                              Murray Gleeson
St Joseph's, North Fitzroy ....Stuart Diver, Bert Newton
St Leo's..Mel Gibson, Michael Duffy
St Patrick's, Ballarat............................George Pell, Steve Moneghetti
St Patrick's, Strathfield ....Tom Keneally, Martin Ferguson
St Peter's ....Howard Florey, Scott Hicks
Star of the Sea ....Germaine Greer, Nicky Buckley
Sydney Boys High ....Russell Crowe, Paddy McGuinness
Sydney Girls High ....Eva Cox, Patricia 'Little Pattie' Amphlett
Sydney Grammar ....Edmund Barton, Siimon Reynolds
Sydney Technical High..................................Robert Askin, Les Gock
Trinity Grammar, Sydney..............................Lonnie Lee, Gavin Long
University High ....Joan Kirner, Olivia Newton-John
Unley High...Julia Gillard, Mark Oliphant
Waverley...Peter Cosgrove, Morris West
Wesley ....Geoffrey Blainey, Poppy King
Xavier...Tim Fisher, Rob De Castella

AUSTRALIAN OLYMPIC BRONZE MEDALLISTS

Olympic Games	Discipline	Event	Name
Paris 1900	Athletics	100m Men	ROWLEY, Stanley
		200m Men	ROWLEY, Stanley
		60m Men	ROWLEY, Stanley
London 1908	Athletics	3500m walk Men	KERR, Harry E.
	Swimming	1500m freestyle Men	BEAUREPAIRE, Frank E.
Stockholm 1912	Swimming	1500m freestyle Men	HARDWICK, Harold H.
		400m freestyle Men	HARDWICK, Harold H.
	Tennis	singles indoor Men	WILDING, Anthony Frederick
Antwerp 1920	Swimming	1500m freestyle Men	BEAUREPAIRE, Frank E.
Paris 1924	Swimming	1500m freestyle Men	BEAUREPAIRE, Frank E.
		400m freestyle Men	CHARLTON, Andrew
Amsterdam 1928	Cycling Track	1km time trial Men	GRAY, Edgar Laurence
Los Angeles 1932	Wrestling Freestyle	79–87kg (light-heavyweight) Men	SCARF, Richard Edward
Berlin 1936	Athletics	triple jump Men	METCALFE, John Patrick
London 1948	Athletics	100m Women	STRICKLAND-DE LA HUNTY, Shirley
		80m hurdles Women	STRICKLAND-DE LA HUNTY, Shirley
	Swimming	100m backstroke Women	DAVIES, Judith Joy
		400m freestyle Men	MARSHALL, John Birnie
	Wrestling Freestyle	+87kg (heavyweight) Men	ARMSTRONG, Joseph
Helsinki 1952	Athletics	100m Women	STRICKLAND-DE LA HUNTY, Shirley
	Rowing	eight with coxswain (8+) Men	TINNING, Robert Noel
			CHAPMAN, Ernest William
			GREENWOOD, Nimrod
			FINLAY, Mervyn David
			PAIN, Edward Oscar
			CAYZER, Phillip Arthur
			CHESSELL, Thomas Edmund
			ANDERSON, David Rollo
			WILLIAMSON, Geoffrey
	Weightlifting	60–67.5kg, total (lightweight) Men	BARBERIS, Verdi

Olympic Games	Discipline	Event	Name
Melbourne/	Athletics	10,000m Men	LAWRENCE, Allan
Stockholm		100m Men	HOGAN, Hector
1956		100m Women	MATHEWS-O'SHEA, Marlene Judith
		1500m Men	LANDY, John
		200m Women	MATHEWS-O'SHEA, Marlene Judith
		80m hurdles Women	THROWER-AUSTIN, Norma Claire
	Boxing	63.5–67kg (welterweight) Men	HOGARTH, Kevin John
	Canoe/Kayak Flatwater	K-2 10,000m Men	GREEN, Dennis Allan BROWN, Walter William
	Cycling Track	Sprint indivual Men	PLOOG, Richard Francis
	Rowing	double sculls (2×) Men	RILEY, Murray Stewart WOOD, Mervyn Thomas
		eight with coxswain (8+) Men	AIKMAN, Michael Hirst BOYKETT, David Herbert BENFIELD, Angus Fred HOWDEN, James Guthrie MANTON, Garth O.V. HOWELL, Walter Neville MONGER, Adrian Calero DOYLE, Brian John HEWITT, Harold Neil
	Sailing	5.5m Mixed	STURROCK, Alexander Stuart MYTTON, Devereaux R. BUXTON, Douglas Raymond
	Swimming	100m freestyle Men	CHAPMAN, Gary
		100m freestyle Women	LEECH, Faith Yvonne
Rome 1960	Athletics	10,000m Men	POWER, David
	Boxing	51–54kg (bantamweight) Men	TAYLOR, Oliver
		75–81kg (light-heavyweight) Men	MADIGAN, Anthony
	Swimming	100m butterfly Women	ANDREW, Janice
		400m freestyle Men	KONRADS, John (Jon)
		4×200m freestyle relay Men	DICKSON, David Gavin DEVITT, John ROSE, Murray KONRADS, John (Jon)

Olympic Games	Discipline	Event	Name
Tokyo 1964	Athletics	10,000m Men	CLARKE, Ronald
		200m Women	BLACK-VASSELLA, Marilyn Mary
		400m Women	AMOORE-POLLOCK, Judith Florence
		80m hurdles Women	KILBORN-RYAN-NELSON, Pamela
	Hockey	Men	DEARING, Paul
			MCWATTERS, Donald
			GLENCROSS, Brian
			MCBRYDE, John
			PEARCE, Julian
			WOOD, Graham
			HODDER, Robin
			EVANS, Raymond
			PEARCE, Eric Robert
			NILAN, Patrick
			SMART, Donald
			CROSSMAN, Mervyn
			PIPER, Desmond
			WATERS, Anthony
	Judo	open category Men	BORONOSKI, Theodore
	Swimming	1500m freestyle Men	WOOD, Allan
		400m freestyle Men	WOOD, Allan
		4×100m freestyle relay Men	DICKSON, David Gavin
			DOAK, Peter John
			RYAN, John
			WINDLE, Robert George
		4×100m medley relay Men	REYNOLDS, Peter Askin
			O'BRIEN, Lawrence Ian
			BERRY, Kevin John
			DICKSON, David Gavin
Mexico 1968	Athletics	200m Women	LAMY-FRANK, Jennifer
	Equestrian/ Eventing	team Mixed	COBCROFT, Brian W.B. DEPECHE
			ROYCROFT, Wayne ZHIVAGO
			ROYCROFT, William WARRATHOOLA
	Swimming	1500m freestyle Men	BROUGH, Gregory
		400m freestyle Women	MORAS, Karen Lynne
		4×100m freestyle relay	ROGERS, Gregory

Olympic Games	Discipline	Event	Name
		Men	CUSACK, Robert
			WINDLE, Robert George
			WENDEN, Michael Vincent
Munich 1972	Swimming	100m breaststroke Women	WHITFIELD, Beverley Joy
		100m freestyle Women	GOULD, Shane
Montreal 1976	Equestrian/ Eventing	team Mixed	ROYCROFT, Wayne
			LAURENSON
			BENNETT, Mervyn
			REGAL REIGN
			ROYCROFT, William
			VERSION
			PIGOTT, Dennis
			HILLSTEAD
	Sailing	double-handed dinghy (470) Men	BROWN, Ian
			RUFF, Ian
		single-handed dinghy (Finn) Men	BERTRAND, John Edwin
	Swimming	1500m freestyle Men	HOLLAND, Stephen
Moscow 1980	Swimming	100m breaststroke Men	EVANS, Peter
		1500m freestyle Men	METZKER, Maxwell
		200m backstroke Men	KERRY, Mark
		200m butterfly Women	FORD, Michelle
		200m freestyle Men	BREWER, Graeme
Los Angeles 1984	Athletics	shot put Women	MULHALL-MARTIN, Gael
	Canoe/Kayak Flatwater	K-2 1000m (kayak double) Men	KELLY, Barry
			KENNY, Grant
	Rowing	eight with coxswain (8+) Men	MULLER, Craig
			HEFER, Clyde
			PATTEN, Samuel
			WILLOUGHBY, Timothy
			EDMUNDS, Ian
			BATTERSBY, James
			POPA, Ion
			EVANS, Stephen
			THREDGOLD, Gavin
	Rowing	four-oared shell with coxswain Women	GREY-GARDNER, Robyn
			BRANCOURT-POLLOCK, Karen
			CHAPMAN-POPA, Susan
			FOSTER, Margot
			LEE, Susan

Olympic Games	Discipline	Event	Name
	Sailing	multihull open (Tornado) Mixed	CAIRNS, Christopher ANDERSON, John Scott
	Shooting	25m pistol (30+30 shots) Women	DENCH, Patricia
	Swimming	100m breaststroke Men	EVANS, Peter
		100m butterfly Men	BUCHANAN, Glenn
		200m individual medley Women	PEARSON, Michelle
		400m freestyle Men	LEMBERG, Justin
		400m individual medley Men	WOODHOUSE, Robert
		4×100m medley relay Men	KERRY, Mark EVANS, Peter BUCHANAN, Glenn STOCKWELL, Marcus
Seoul 1988	Canoe/Kayak Flatwater	K-2 1000m (kayak double) Men	FOSTER, Peter GRAHAM, Kelvin John
	Cycling Track	Sprint individual Men	NEIWAND, Garry Malcolm
		Team Pursuit (4000m) Men	DUTTON, Brett MCCARNEY, Wayne MCGLEDE, Stephen John WOODS, Dean
	Swimming	800m freestyle Women	MCDONALD, Julie
	Tennis	doubles Women	SMYLIE, Elizabeth TURNBULL, Wendy
Barcelona 1992	Athletics	discus throw Women	COSTIAN, Daniela
	Athletics	high jump Men	FORSYTH, Timothy
	Canoe/Kayak Flatwater	K-4 1000m (kayak four) Men	ANDERSSON, Ramon Dean GRAHAM, Kelvin John ROWLING, Ian Mark WOOD, Steven Michael
	Sailing	board (lechner) Men	KLEPPICH, Lars Detlef
		multihull open (Tornado) Mixed	BOOTH, Mitch FORBES, John Robert
	Swimming	100m breaststroke Men	ROGERS, Philip John
		100m breaststroke Women	RILEY, Samantha Linette
		200m backstroke Women	STEVENSON, Nicole Dawn
		200m butterfly Women	O'NEILL, Susan
		400m freestyle Women	LEWIS, Hayley Jane

Olympic Games	Discipline	Event	Name
	Tennis	doubles Women	MCQUILLAN, Rachel Jane
			BRADTKE, Nicole Anne Louise
Lillehammer 1994	Short Track Speed Skating	5000m relay Men	BRADBURY, Steven
			HANSEN, Kieran
			MURTHA, Andrew
			NIZIELSKI, Richard
Atlanta 1996	Basketball	Women	MAHER, Robyn
			COOK, Allison
			BRONDELLO, Alexandra
			TIMMS, Michelle
			SANDIE, Shelley
			FALLON, Trisha
			CHANDLER, Michelle
			ROBINSON, Fiona
			BOYD, Carla
			WHITTLE, Jennifer
			SPORN, Rachael
			BROGAN, Michelle
	Beach volleyball	Women	COOK, Natalie
			POTTHARST, Kerri Ann
	Canoe/Kayak Flatwater	K-1 1000m (kayak single) Men	ROBINSON, Clint
		K-2 500m (kayak double) Men	TRIM, Andrew Lawrence
			COLLINS, Daniel James
		K-2 500m (kayak double) Women	WOOD, Anna Maria
			BORCHERT, Katrin
	Cycling Track	Individual Pursuit Men	MCGEE, Bradley
		points race Men	O'GRADY, Stuart Peter
		points race Women	TYLER SHARMAN, Lucy
		Team Pursuit (4000m) Men	AITKEN, Brett
			O'GRADY, Stuart Peter
			O'SHANNESSEY, Timothy
			WOODS, Dean

Olympic Games	Discipline	Event	Name
	Hockey	Men	HAGER, Marcus
			DAVIES, Stephen
			CHOPPY, Baeden
			ELMER, Lachlan
			CARRUTHERS, Stuart
			SMITH, Grant
			DILETTI, Damon
			DREHER, Lachlan
			GARARD, Brendan
			GAUDOIN, Paul
			LEWIS, Paul Snowden
			SMITH, Matthew
			STACEY, Jay Jason
			SPROULE, Daniel
			WARK, Kenneth
			YORK, Michael
	Rowing	lightweight double sculls (2×) Men	HICK, Bruce
			EDWARDS, Anthony
		lightweight double sculls (2×) Women	LEE, Virginia
			JOYCE, Rebecca
		quadruple sculls without cox Men	HOOKER, Janusz
			HANSON, Boden Joseph
			FREE, Duncan
			SNOOK, Ronald
	Sailing	two-person keelboat open (Star) Mixed	BEASHEL, Colin Kenneth
			GILES, David James
	Shooting	double trap (120 targets) Women	HUDDLESTON, Deserie
	Softball	Women	BROWN, Joanne
			COOPER, Kim
			CRUDGINGTON, Carolyn
			DIENELT, Kerry
			EDEBONE, Peta
			HARDING, Tanya
			HOLLIDAY, Jennifer
			LESTER, Jocelyn
			MCDERMID, Sally
			MCRAE, Francine
			PETRIE, Haylea
			RICHARDSON, Nicole
			ROCHE, Melanie
			WARD, Natalie
			WILKINS, Brooke

Olympic Games	Discipline	Event	Name
	Swimming	100m breaststroke Women	RILEY, Samantha Linette
		200m butterfly Men	GOODMAN, Scott
		200m freestyle Men	KOWALSKI, Daniel
		400m freestyle Men	KOWALSKI, Daniel
		4×100m medley relay Men	DEWICK, Steven
			ROGERS, Philip John
			MILLER, Scott
			KLIM, Michael
		4×200m freestyle relay Women	GREVILLE, Julia
			STEVENSON, Nicole Dawn
			JOHNSON, Emma
			O'NEILL, Susan
	Weightlifting	+ 108kg, total (super heavyweight) Men	BOTEV, Stefan
Nagano 1998	Alpine Skiing	slalom Women	STEGGALL, Zali
Sydney 2000	Canoe/Kayak Flatwater	K-1 500m (kayak single) Women	BORCHERT, Katrin
	Cycling Track	1km time trial Men	KELLY, Shane John
		Individual Pursuit Men	MCGEE, Bradley
		Olympic Sprint Men	NEIWAND, Garry Malcolm
			EADIE, Sean
			HILL, Darryn
	Diving	synchronized diving 10m platform Women	GILMORE, Rebecca
			TOURKY, Loudy
		synchronized diving 3m springboard Men	NEWBERY, Robert
			PULLAR, Dean
	Hockey	Men	DAVIES, Stephen
			GAUDOIN, Paul
			SPROULE, Daniel
			YORK, Michael
			STACEY, Jay Jason
			DILETTI, Damon
			DREHER, Lachlan
			BRENNAN, Michael
			COMMENS, Adam
			DUFF, Jason
			ELDER, Troy
			ELMER, James
			HOLT, Stephen
			LIVERMORE, Brent
			VICTORY, Craig
			WELLS, Matthew

Olympic Games	Discipline	Event	Name
	Judo	52–57kg (lightweight) Women	PEKLI, Maria
	Rowing	coxless pair (2–) Men	LONG, Matthew
			TOMKINS, James
	Rowing	four without coxswain (4–) Men	STEWART, James
			DODWELL, Ben Philip
			STEWART, Geoffrey
			HANSON, Boden Joseph
	Sailing	single-handed dinghy open (Laser) Mixed	BLACKBURN, Michael
	Shooting	10m air pistol (40 shots) Women	FORDER, Annemarie
	Softball	Women	BROWN, Joanne
			DIENELT, Kerry
			EDEBONE, Peta
			HARDING, Tanya
			ROCHE, Melanie
			WARD, Natalie
			WILKINS, Brooke
			ALLEN, Sandra
			FAIRHURST, Sue
			FOLLAS, Selina
			HANES, Fiona
			HARDIE, Kelly
			MCDERMID, Sally
			MORROW, Simmone
			TITCUME, Natalie
	Swimming	100m butterfly Men	HUEGILL, Geoff
		200m backstroke Men	WELSH, Matthew
		200m butterfly Men	NORRIS, Justin
		200m butterfly Women	THOMAS, Petria
Athens 2004	Archery	individual Men	CUDDIHY, Tim
	Athletics	20km walk Men	DEAKES, Nathan
		20km walk Women	SAVILLE, Jane
	Cycling Track	Keirin Men	KELLY, Shane
		Sprint Women	MEARES, Anna
	Diving	10m platform Women	TOURKY, Loudy
		Synchronised 3m springboard Men	BARNETT, Steven
			NEWBERY, Robert
		Synchronised 3m springboard Women	LASHKO, Irina
			NEWBERY, Chantelle
		Synchronised 10 m platform Men	HELM, Mathew
			NEWBERY, Robert

Olympic Games	Discipline	Event	Name
	Rowing	quadruple sculls Women	BRADLEY, Amber
			FALETIC, Dana
			HORE, Kerry
			SATTIN, Rebecca
		eight with coxswain (8+) Men	SZCZUROWSKI, Stefan
			RESIDE, Stuart
			WELCH, Stuart
			STEWART, James
			STEWART, Geoff
			STEWART, Steve
			HANSON, Boden
			MCKAY, Mike
			TOON, Michael
	Shooting	Trap Men	VELLA, Adam
	Swimming	50m freestyle Women	LENTON, Lisbeth
		100m breastrtroke Women	JONES, Liesel
		100m freestyle Men	THORPE, Ian
	Tennis	singles Women	MOLIK, Alicia

PROMINENT AUSTRALIANS WITH DISABILITIES

Billy Hughes	*prime minister*	deaf
Roden Cutler VC	*governor of NSW*	lost foot in World War II
Jack Newton	*golfer*	lost eye and arm in light plane accident
Louise Sauvage	*paralympian*	myelodysplasia, scoliosis
John Cornforth	*Nobel prize winner 1975*	deaf

Note: While not technically disabled, John Gorton (prime minister 1968–71) suffered severe facial injuries during his World War II RAAF service. However, these may actually have helped his political career by making his face more recognisable.

'THE ASHES'

Held at Lord's, the trophy of the Australia–England cricket series is a small urn said to hold the ashes of a burnt bail.

AUSTRALIAN ICONS

After quoting D. H. Lawrence's description of a war memorial in his novel *Kangaroo*, the historian K. S. Inglis in his book *Sacred Places: War Memorials in the Australian Landscape* (Melbourne, 1998) says that 'Lawrence had discovered an Australian icon. For once the word can be used with no stretch of meaning: a bodily image, created to be revered'.

With varying degrees of stretching, the following people and things have been called 'Australian Icons', or at least 'iconic':

The Sydney Harbour Bridge
The Sydney Opera House
The Akubra hat
Uluru
The kangaroo
Aeroplane Jelly
Aspro
The blue heeler
Chesty Bond
Ginger Meggs
The Gumnut Babies
The Hills Hoist
The Holden car
Jaffas
The kelpie
The Kokoda Track
Lifesavers
The meat pie
The Melbourne Cup
Minties
The Bong Bong Picnic Races
Qantas
The Twelve Apostles, Victoria
The ute
Vegemite
The Victa mower

The Violet Crumble
Slim Dusty
Jimmy Little
The Pinnacles, WA
Don Bradman
Joan Sutherland
John Flynn
Burke and Wills
Kylie Minogue
The Flying Doctor
The koala
The crocodile
The Eureka flag
Phar Lap
Ned Kelly
The outdoor dunny
The boomerang
The didgeridoo
The gum tree
The Great Barrier Reef
The FJ Holden
The Ghan
Telstra
Richie Benaud
Ian Chappell
The stump jump plough

Penfolds Grange Hermitage
Blinky Bill
Paul Hogan
Edna Everage
The pavlova
The Driza-Bone
The barbie
The merino
The Mambo shirt
Lowitja O'Donoghue
Waltzing Matilda
The Jackie Howe singlet
The Melbourne W-class tram
Mental as Anything
Men at Work
Tim Tams
Cricket
Splayds
The Go-Betweens
Hayley Lewis
The Australian War Memorial
The beach
Betty Cuthbert
'Weary' Dunlop
The Bush
Smith's Crisps
Bega cheese
The RMB (Roadside Mail Box)
Anne Geddes photographs
Arnott's biscuits
Charles Kingsford-Smith
The Anzacs
Daisy Bates

State of Origin
The 'Tea and Sugar' Train
R. M. Williams (the man and the clothing)
Humphey B. Bear
The Southern Cross
The 'Southern Cross' windmill
Smokey Dawson
Aboriginal 'dot' painting
The Magic Pudding
Skippy
The Aboriginal flag
The 'Jason' recliner-rocker
Louie the Fly
Germaine Greer
Gough Whitlam
The Snowy Mountains Hydroelectric Scheme
The Blundstone boot
Kakadu
The Australian magpie
The Australian Post Office
The outback homestead
John Williamson
Barry Jones
Fairness
Max Dupain's *Sunbaker*
Ted Whitten
The Holden Sandman
Henry Lawson
Nineteenth century landscape painting
'Breaker' Morant

APOLLO TRACKING STATIONS IN AUSTRALIA

Honeysuckle Creek, ACT
One of three stations worldwide (others at Goldstone, California and Fresnedillas, Madrid, Spain) to communicate with and track Apollo spacecraft during lunar orbits, landing and return.
Contains 26 m antenna.

Tidbinbilla, ACT
'Wing station' to Honeysuckle Creek.
Contains 26 m antenna. In 1972 a 64 m (later 70 m) antenna added, first operational role to support Apollo 17.

Parkes, NSW
64 m radio telescope, assisted during Apollo 11 (1969) and the Apollo 13 emergency (1970). However, the Apollo 11 television pictures came to Earth through Honeysuckle Creek, not Parkes (as in the 2000 film *The Dish*).

Carnarvon, WA
9 m antenna communicated with astronauts during near-Earth phase of missions.

THE FELTON BEQUEST

On his death in 1904, Alfred Felton left £378,033 (the equivalent of $40,000,000 today) to art and charity, with half the interest to be used to buy works for the National Gallery of Victoria. Felton had made his fortune as a merchant and pharmaceuticals manufacturer after arriving in Melbourne from England in 1853. His bequest gave the NGV acquisition funds greater than those of London's National and Tate galleries combined. About 15,000 works of art have been bought with the bequest, includes works by Rembrandt, William Blake, Tiepolo, Monet, Cézanne, van Gogh and Turner. Their value is estimated at more than $1 billion.

UNDERGROUND RAILWAY STATIONS

Sydney

Central (part)	Mascot
Town Hall	Domestic
Wynyard	International
St James	Wolli Creek
Museum	**Melbourne**
Redfern (part)	Flinders St (part)
Martin Place	Spencer St (part)
Kings Cross	Flagstaff
Edgecliff	Melbourne Central
Bondi Junction	Parliament
Green Square	**Brisbane**
	Central

IRREGULAR POSTCODES

Generally, the following Postcode ranges are allocated to the states/territories:

NSW, ACT	2000–2999
Vic	3000–3999
Qld	4000–4999
SA	5000–5999
WA	6000–6999
Tas	7000–7499
NT	0800–0899

The following postcodes are outside these ranges:

A'Beckett Street PO Boxes, Vic	8006
Alexandria PO Boxes, NSW	1435
Ashfield PO Boxes, NSW	1800
Auburn PO Boxes, NSW	1835
Australia Square PO Boxes, NSW	1215
Baulkham Hills PO Boxes, NSW	1755

Milsons Point PO Boxes, NSW 1565
Miranda PO Boxes, NSW 1490
Mona Vale PO Boxes, NSW 1660
Moorebank PO Boxes, NSW 1875
North Parramatta PO Boxes, NSW.................1750
Northbridge PO Boxes, NSW 1560
Pennant Hills PO Boxes, NSW 1715
Potts Point PO Boxes, NSW 1335
Queen Victoria Building PO Boxes, NSW 1230
Rosebery PO Boxes, NSW 1445
Royal Exchange PO Boxes, NSW 1225
Rydalmere BC PO Boxes, NSW 1701
Ryde PO Boxes, NSW....................................1680
Seven Hills PO Boxes, NSW 1730
Silverwater PO Boxes, NSW 1811
St Kilda Road PO Boxes, Vic 8004
St Kilda Road Central PO Boxes, Vic 8008
St Leonards PO Boxes, NSW 1590
St Marys PO Boxes, NSW 1790
Sutherland PO Boxes, NSW.............................1499
Sydney South PO Boxes, NSW 1235
UNSW Sydney PO Boxes, NSW 1466
West Chatswood PO Boxes, NSW 1515
West Ryde PO Boxes, NSW 1685
Wetherill Park DC PO Boxes, NSW................1851
Woollahra PO Boxes, NSW 1350
World Trade Centre PO Boxes, Vic.................8005

FIVE AUSTRALIAN POSTAL FIRSTS

1. First post office: Sydney, 1809
2. First pre-paid postage (world first): 1838
3. First pictorial postage stamp (world first): Sydney 1849
4. First stated commemorative stamp (world first): NSW, 1888
5. First airmail service: 1914 (between Sydney and Melbourne)

LIVING TREASURES

The National Trust's Living Treasures Committee announced its list of 100 'Australian Living Treasures' in 1997, honouring people deemed to have added lasting attributes to Australia's culture and heritage. It has since been revised following the death of 15 of the original Living Treasures.

Phillip Adams AO
Betty Archdale MBE*
Dr Faith Bandler AM
Her Excellency Professor
Marie Bashir AC
John Bell AM OBE
Prof Geoffrey Blainey AO
Arthur Boyd AC OBE*
Raelene Boyle MBE
Sir Donald Bradman AC*
The Rev Father Frank
Brennan AO
Senator Bob Brown
Julian Burnside
Don Burrows AO MBE
Evonne Cawley AO MBE
The Rev Tim Costello
Ruth Cracknell AM*
The Rev Bill Crews AM
Russell Crowe
Bart Cummings AM
Betty Cuthbert AM MBE
Sir Roden Cutler VC, AK,
KCMG, KStJ, KCVO, CBE*
Judy Davis
His Excellency the Hon Sir
William Deane AC KBE
Ernie Dingo AM
Dr Michael James Dodson AM
Pat Dodson

Prof Peter Doherty AC
The Hon Don Dunstan AC*
Slim Dusty AO MBE*
Ted Egan
The Hon Justice Marcus
Einfeld AO QC
Herb Elliott AC MBE
John Farnham AO
Dawn Fraser AO MBE
The Hon Malcolm Fraser
AC CH
Cathy Freeman OAM
Margaret Fulton OAM
Peter Garrett AM
Jennie George
Shane Gould MBE
Dr Germaine Greer
Dr Catherine Hamlin
Rolf Harris AM OBE
John Hatton AO
Hazel Hawke AO
Dr Basil Hetzel AC
The Most Rev Peter
Hollingworth AO OBE
Gabi Hollows
Janet Holmes à Court AO
Donald Horne AO*
The Hon John Howard
Robert Hughes AO
Barry Humphries AO

Elizabeth Jolley AO
The Hon Barry Jones AO
Caroline Jones AO
The Hon Paul Keating
Thomas Keneally AO
Cheryl Kernot
Nicole Kidman
Ian Kiernan AO OAM
The Hon Justice Michael
Kirby AC CMG
Prof Dame Leonie Kramer
AC DBE
His Excellency John Landy
AC MBE
Rod Laver
Michael Leunig
Jimmy Little
Ted Mack
David Malouf AO
Ted Matthews*
Dr Colleen McCullough
Garry McDonald AO
Walter Mikac
Dr Jack Mundey AO
Graeme Murphy AM
Les Murray AO
John Newcombe AO OBE
Greg Norman AM
Sir Gustav Nossal AC CBE
Dr Lowitja O'Donoghue AC
CBE AM
Dr Pat O'Shane AM
Sir Mark Oliphant AC*
Dr Margaret Olley AO
Mary Paton

Noel Pearson
Charles Perkins AO*
Kieren Perkins OAM
Pat Rafter
Prof Henry A. Reynolds
Ken Rosewall
Prof Peter Sculthorpe AO OBE
Dick Smith AO
Mum (Shirl) Smith AM MBE*
Professor Fiona Stanley
Dame Joan Sutherland OM
AC DBE
Mavis Taylor
Richard Tognetti
The Hon Tom Uren AO
The Rev Sir Alan Walker Kt
OBE DD*
Nancy Bird-Walton AO OBE
Anthony Warlow
Gai Waterhouse
Steve Waugh
Morris West AO*
The Hon Gough Whitlam
AC QC
Margaret Whitlam AO
R. M. Williams AO CMG*
Robyn Williams AM
David Williamson AO
Tim Winton
Dr Fiona Wood AM
Roger Woodward AC OBE
Judith Wright McKinney*
Dr John Yu AC
Galarrwuy Yunupingu AM

* Deceased (Donald Horne died as we went to press)

DON'T MISS THESE EVENTS

NSW

January	Gunnedah	National Tomato Competition
	Parkes	Elvis Revival
February	Temora	Golden Gift foot race
March	Bega	Cheese Pro-Am
	Jindabyne	Strzelecki Polish Festival
	Lismore	Square Dance Festival
	Wellington	The Wellington Boot horse races
Easter	Corowa	Billy Cart Races
	Gilgandra	Goat Races
	Grenfell	Guinea Pig Races
	Lightning Ridge	Great Goat Race
	Moulamein	Yabby Races
April	Milton	Scarecrow Festival
May	Macksville	Egg-throwing Championships; Trek to the 'pub-with-no-beer'
	Nimbin	Mardi Grass [sic] Festival
June	Grenfell	Henry Lawson Festival of Arts; Guinea Pig Races
	Nambucca Heads	Ken Howard Memorial Bowls Competition
July	Stroud	International Brick and Rolling-pin Throwing
August	Menindee	Burke and Wills Fishing Challenge
	Murwillumbah	Tweed Valley Banana Festival
	Nambucca Heads	VW Spectacular (odd-numbered years)
September	Batlow	Daffodil Show
	Henty	Machinery Field Days
	Newcastle	Hamilton Fiesta
October	Kundabung	Australasian Bull-riding Titles
November	Albury	Festival of the Bogong Moth

	Barraba	Barrarbor (celebrating music and trees)
	Blackheath	Rhododendron Festival
	Bombala	Fairground Organ Festival
December	Abercrombie Caves	Carols in the Caves

Victoria

January	Ballarat	Organs of the Ballarat Goldfields
	Blackwood	Shindig Festival
	Hoddles Creek	Upper Yarra Draught Horse Festival
February	Seymour	Alternative Farming Expo
March	Erica	King of the Mountain Woodchop
	Korumburra	Karmai (giant worm) Festival
	Myrtleford	Tobacco, Hops and Timber Festival
Easter	Quambatook	Australian Tractor Pull Championship
	Wonthaggi	Coal Skip Fill
	Winghnu	Tractor Pull Festival
April	Geelong	Alternative Farmvision
May	Kalorama	Chestnut Festival
July	Camperdown	One Act Play Festival
August	Hamilton	Sheepvention
October	Cobram	Sun Country Dolls, Bears and Collectables Show
	Harrietville	Ride-on Mower Grand Prix
December	Bendigo	Tram Spectacular

Queensland

February	Chinchilla	Melon Festival (odd-numbered years)
March	Gin Gin	Wild Scotchman Festival
Easter	Warwick	Rock Swap

April	Kingaroy	Peanut Festival (odd-numbered years)
May	Gatton	Heavy Horse Field Days
	Noosa	Hot and Spicy Food Festival
June	Emerald	Wheelbarrow Derby (odd-numbered years)
	Mundubbera	Citrus Celebration Week
	Muttaburra	Landsborough Flock Ewe Show
July	Hughenden	Dinosaur Festival (even-numbered years)
	Karumba	Karumba Kapers
August	Yeppoon	World Cooeeing Festival
September	Eulo	World Lizard Racing Championships
October	Crows Nest	Worm Races

South Australia

January	Port Germein	Festival of the Crab
February	Mount Compass	Cow Race
Easter	Jamestown	Bilby Hunt
May	Mannum	Houseboat Hirers' Open Days
July	Maree	Australian Camel Cup
	Woomera	4th of July Celebrations
August	Port Augusta	Camel Cup
October	McLaren Vale	Continuous Picnic
November	Strathalbyn	Duck Race
	Streaky Bay	Camel Cup

Western Australia

January	Denmark	Pantomime in Berridge Park
	Fremantle	Sardine Festival
March	Carnamah	Wimbledon of the Wheatbelt
	Narrogin	Agrolympics
Easter	Lancelin	Beach Buggy Championships
April	Exmouth	Billfish Bonanza

May	Gingin	British Car Day
June	Geraldton	Batavia Celebrations
August	Badgingarra	Shears Competition
	Karratha	FeNaClNG Festival*
	Katanning	Prophet Mohammed's Birthday
	Tom Price	Nameless Festival
September	Beverley	Duck Race
October	Northampton	Airing of the Quilts
November	Broome	Mango Festival
	Fitzroy Crossing	Barra Splash
December	Katanning	Caboodle

Tasmania

January	Triabunna	Spring Bay Crayfish Derby
February	Evandale	Village Fair and National Penny Farthing Championships
	Waratah	Axemen's Carnival
March	New Norfolk	Hop Harvest Festival
August	Ulverstone	Doll, Toy and Miniature Fair

ACT

July	Canberra	ANU Chess Festival
September–October	Canberra	Floriade
December–January	Canberra	Street Machine Summernats (national hot-rod exhibition and races)

Northern Territory

July	Alice Springs	Camel Cup
August	Darwin	Beer Can Regatta
October	Alice Springs	Henley-on-Todd Regatta

* FeNaClNG stands for Fe[Iron]NaCl[Salt]NG[Natural Gas].

THE 'TABLECLOTH'

The 1999 NSW elections saw a Legislative Council ballot paper with 264 candidates in 81 groups distributed across three rows on a ballot paper approximately one metre across by 70 centimetres down. The parties on it, in descending order of votes cast, were:

1 Australian Labor Party
2 Liberal/National Party
3 Pauline Hanson's One Nation
4 Australian Democrats
5 Christian Democratic Party (Fred Nile Group)
6 The Greens
7 John Tingle – The Shooters Party
8 Progressive Labor Party
9 Marijuana Smokers Rights Party
10 Reform the Legal System
11 Unity
12 Country Summit Alliance
13 Registered Clubs Party
14 Gun Owners & Sporting Hunters Rights
15 Country Party
16 What's Doing? Party
17 A Better Future For Our Children
18 Franca Arena Child Safety Alliance
19 Three Day Weekend Party
20 Australian Family Alliance
21 Young Australians Caring for our Future
22 Australians Against Further Immigration
23 Gay and Lesbian Party
24 Australians Against the Promotion of Homosexuality
25 The Australian Small Business Party
26 Animal Liberation Party
27 Democratic Socialists
28 Speranza: Hope for Better Health NSW
29 The Four Wheel Drive Party
30 Outdoor Recreation Party
31 Riders' and Motorists' Party
32 Kevin Ryan – Drug Reform
33 The Seniors Party
34 Jobs for Everyone – Futures for All
35 Marine Environment Conservation Party
36 The Wilderness Party
37 Stop Banks from Exploiting Australians Group
38 Australian Independents Coalition for Political Integrity
39 Fair Tax Party
40 Help Disabled People
41 No GST/Mick Gallagher for Australia

42 NSW Ratepayers Party
43 Womens Party/Save the Forests
44 Australia First
45 Make Billionaires Pay More Tax!
46 Euthanasia Referendum Party
47 Care For Us Party
48 (Godfrey Bigot) People Before Party Politics
49 Hospitals, Education, Law, Privacy
50 Earthsave
51 People Against Paedophiles
52 Independent Community Network
53 Abolish State Governments!
54 A Fair Go For Families
55 Communist Party of Australia
56 Voice of the People Party
57 Citizens Electoral Councils of Australia (NSW)
58 Natural Law Party
59 Give Criminals Longer Sentences
60 Responsible Drug Reform for Australia
61 Republic 2001/People First

62 Outside Newcastle Sydney Wollongong Party
63 Responsible Gambling Party
64 No Nuclear Waste Dumps Party
65 Motor Vehicle Consumer Protection Party
66 No Privatisation Peoples Party
67 No Badgerys Creek Airport Party
68 Independent (Esposito)
69 Anti-Corruption Party (Insurers, Lawyers, Politicians)
70 Non-Custodial Parents Party
71 Elect The President
72 Australians for a Better Community
73 Reclaim Australia
74 Our Common Future Party
75 Independent (Kanan)
76 Hotel Patrons Party
77 Reform Parliamentary Superannuation Party
78 Community First Party
79 The Timbarra Clean Water Party
80 Tenants Have Rights
81 Ungrouped candidates

THE CLARKS AND AUSTRALIA

Kenneth Clark (1903–1983), later Lord Clark of *Civilisation* fame, visited Australia in 1939 while Director of Britain's National Gallery. He later described Australia as 'that intolerable continent' and said Australian galleries had the worst art, but the best Victorian pornography, in the world.

The Clark family wealth came from Clark's Cotton Thread in Paisley, Scotland (Kenneth Clark's great-great-grandfather invented the cotton spool) and the family owned a series of yachts called *Katoomba*. The name came from a visit by Clark's father to Australia in his teens.

Lord Clark's son Alan (1928–1999), a historian and Conservative politician, wrote the first of his (in)famous *Diaries* in an old visitors book from one of the yachts, which he had found in the library at the Clark home, Saltwood Castle in Kent. It was bound in crimson leather with the word 'Katoomba' in gold leaf on the front: 'It seems appropriate enough for the new set of journals – Katoomba has long been an evocative name for me.'

WHY KOALAS SUFFER FROM CHLAMYDIA

When the Britsh journalist A. A. Gill heard that koalas suffer from this sexually transmitted disease, he exclaimed, 'My God, you Australians will have a go at anything!'

But it's not what you think, Mr Gill. Scientists now believe that chlamydia has occurred among koala populations for many years. Usually dormant, it is triggered by times of stress (such as when koala habitat is reduced). Symptoms of koala chlamydia include sore eyes, chest infections, and 'wet bottom' or 'dirty tail'. Weaker koalas die or become sick or infertile, leaving the stronger ones to continue breeding. Chlamydia thus acts as a natural form of koala population control.

CHARLES DICKENS AND AUSTRALIA

References to Australia recur throughout the work of Dickens. At the end of *David Copperfield*, the Micawbers emigrate and do well, with Mr Micawber eventually becoming a magistrate. In *Great Expectations*, Magwitch the convict is transported to Australia, and after serving his sentence makes his fortune, which he uses to turn Pip into a gentleman.

Dickens had personal links with Australia: his sons Alfred D'Orsay Tennyson Dickens (1845–1912) and Edward Bulwer Lytton Dickens (1852–1902) both emigrated to Australia. His father called Alfred 'a good, steady, fellow', but had doubts about his youngest child Edward, nicknamed 'Plorn'. When Plorn also left for Australia at the age of sixteen another son, Henry, said he 'never saw a man so completely overcome' as his father when seeing Plorn off from Paddington station.

After initial success in business (and Plorn becoming a member of the NSW Parliament) both sons fell on hard times. Plorn died poor in 1902, and Alfred survived by giving public lectures about his father. These proved a success, and he gave them in Australia and overseas, dying in New York in 1912. His Australian-born daughters emigrated to Britain in the 1920s.

But there was a further Dickens link. In 1960 his great-granddaughter the novelist Monica Dickens (1915–1992) was in a Sydney bookstore autographing her books when a woman held out a book to her and said, 'Emma chisit'. Thinking this to be the woman's name, she wrote 'To Emma Chisit' on the flyleaf. 'Nah', said the woman, '*emma chisit*?' She was in fact asking: 'How much is it?' 'Strine' was born.

THE 'BALL OF THE CENTURY'

In 1993 Aussie leg spinner Shane Warne stunned the cricketing world when he bowled English captain Mike Gatting with his first ball in a Test match in England.

THOSE LATHAMS

John

Born 1877, he was head of Australian Naval Intelligence during World War I and attended the Versailles Peace Conference. Elected to the House of Representatives as an independent, he later joined the Nationalist Party and became leader after its defeat in 1929. When Joseph Lyons went over from Labor in 1931, Latham gave way to him as leader of the new conservative United Australia Party: the tall, aloof Latham lacked his personal magnetism. After being Attorney-General and External Affairs minister, he became Chief Justice of the High Court 1935–1952. He was briefly first Australian minister to Japan, 1940–41. In the 1950s he was the only High Court judge to support Robert Menzies' attempt to ban the Communist Party. An atheist and rationalist all his life, he died in 1964.

Noel

In 1977, Broken Hill City Council employee Noel Latham was fined by the Barrier Industrial Council, the peak union organisation which effectively ran the town. He had informed on another union member on a safety issue, an act which broke a longstanding BIC rule. He refused to pay, and lost his job after unionists refused to work with him. He took the workers to court, winning $70,000 in damages.

Mark

Born 1961, he grew up in Green Valley in Sydney's western suburbs, attending Hurlstone Agricultural High School. He completed a Bachelor of Economics degree (Honours) at Sydney University in 1982. He was a councillor on Liverpool City Council between 1987 and 1994 and mayor from 1991 to 1994. He was elected to the House of Representatives as Member for Werriwa (Gough Whitlam's old seat) at a by-election in 1994. He wrote several books on policy, including *Civilising Global Capital* (1998). Elected to the Shadow Ministry in 2001, he became leader of the Federal Parliamentary

Labor Party in 2003. His insults included 'conga line of suckholes'. He resigned as Leader and Member for Werriwa in January 2005, citing ill-health.

Chris
Born in 1975 in Narrabri, he first played rugby for Queensland in 1998, and made his test debut against France the same year. He won the Pilecki medal for Queensland player of the year in 1999, 2000, 2002, and 2004, and Australian Super 12 Player of the Year in 2000, 2003 and 2004. He lost his place at full-back in the 2003 World Cup to the former rugby league player Mat Rogers, but Rogers' injury meant he regained it for the 2004 Tri-Nations series against New Zealand and South Africa.

None of these Lathams are related.

VIENNA MOZART BOYS' CHOIR, 1939

The Vienna Mozart Boys' Choir (a breakaway from the Vienna Boys' Choir) was on a nine-month world tour in 1939, which ended in Australia. They were in Fremantle awaiting transportation home when World War II broke out. The twenty boys, aged nine to fourteen, and their choirmaster were stranded in Australia as enemy aliens: the previous year, Austria had been absorbed into Hitler's Germany.

Daniel Mannix, Catholic Archbishop of Melbourne, offered the boys places in the newly-formed St Patrick's Cathedral Boys' Choir, as well as foster homes in Melbourne and education at Christian Brothers College, East Melbourne.

All but one of the boys stayed on in Australia after the war. One of them, Stefan Haag, eventually became an opera and theatre director, who recommended to Harry M. Miller that he bring the musical *Hair* to Australia.

POPULAR AUSSIE WHINGES

In the opening credits of Universal Studios films, Australia being the only permanently inhabited continent not seen on the globe.

Getting treated like aliens by British immigration officers at Heathrow Airport while their new German friends waltz in.

Being mistaken for Austrians.

Being mistaken for New Zealanders/Canadians/South Africans/English/Americans.

The phrase 'Australian culture' being regarded as a contradiction of terms.

Having to remind people that the 2000 Olympics were held in Australia.

All those big-name Australian actors and directors not making Australian films any more.

MORGAN'S MIGHT-HAVE-BEENS

1. Endeavour sinks on Great Barrier Reef, 1770

Having run aground, the *Endeavour* proved unsalvageable. Captain James Cook and his crew made for shore in the ship's boats with as much of the ships' provisions as they could load. Realising that their chances of rescue were practically nil, Cook then decided to try to reach Timor, as William Bligh was to do in a longboat nineteen years later after the *Bounty* mutiny. Cook succeeded, and all but one of the crew survived: before the longboat left, the ship's botanist, Joseph Banks, was speared by a native while examining what came to be known as a banksia. Banks was thus unable to make the case to the British government for establishing a penal colony in Australia. France established a colony instead, and Britain felt compelled to follow, leading to a 'scramble for Australia' and sporadic wars between French and British Australia which continued for decades, until France finally won control and renamed the continent Nouvelle Hollande. In 1971 the French caused an international furore when they let off nuclear devices on Ile Napoleon (known to the British as Lord Howe Island). That year's Bonaparte Cup rugby competition between the New Zealand All Blacks and the Nouvelle Hollande Ouallabies was marred by ugly brawls both on and off the field.

2. Ned Kelly escapes Glenrowan, 1880

Hiding out in the bush, Ned outlived Judge Redmond Barry. He was finally caught and tried in 1881. The jury returned a verdict of manslaughter (which Judge Barry would have told them they could not do) and so Kelly avoided martyrdom. Freed some years later, he told reporters: 'I fought for what I believed was right'. He emigrated to the United States, where he supported himself by giving dramatic and very popular lectures about his exploits.

3. Henry Parkes falls off the train at Tenterfield, 1889

Sir Henry Parkes, Premier of NSW, was on his way back to Sydney from Brisbane when he stopped at Tenterfield, the electorate he represented in NSW Parliament. But instead of delivering the 'Tenterfield Oration' regarded as the start of the move toward Federation, Parkes tripped and fell as he got off the train, hitting his head and eventually succumbing to his injuries after never regaining consciousness. The Australian colonies remained separate (although co-operating in areas such as defence) for another thirty years. The continued isolation of WA, due to the lack of a transcontinental railway, meant that it refused to join. It remains separate to this day.

4. Pte Bruce Kingsbury VC isn't at Isurava, 1942

In 1942, Bruce Kingsbury was a 24-year-old real estate agent from Melbourne. When war broke out in 1939 he and his mate Alan Avery had joined up together, but found themselves in separate units: Bruce in the 2/2nd Pioneers and Alan in the 2/14th Infantry.

They tossed a coin over who would apply for a transfer, but instead of Bruce going into the 2/14th (and winning a posthumous Victoria Cross for his heroism in leading a charge that repelled the Japanese at Isurava on the Kokoda Track in 1942) Alan went into the Pioneers, and both spent the war as prisoners in Singapore. Bruce was thus unable to lead a charge against the Japanese who were poised to overrun the 2/14th's battalion headquarters. It fell, and so did Port Moresby, enabling the Japanese to use New Guinea as a base for raids on Australia. The successful conquest of New Guinea strengthened the hand of General Yamashita in calling for an invasion, and Japanese forces came ashore near Brisbane and Sydney in October 1942. In bitter fighting, the Australians repelled them, and Battle of Noosa Day and Battle of Woy Woy Day are now national holidays.

5. Harold Holt doesn't drown off Portsea

At Portsea on the morning of December 17, 1967, Harold Holt was about to go for a swim when he received a telephone call from his office. After being detained for fifteen minutes he finally joined a group of friends on Cheviot Beach. However before he could enter the water, Holt suffered a mild heart attack. An ambulance rushed him to hospital where he made a full recovery but doubts about his health persisted, contributing to his loss in the 1969 election. Gough Whitlam's victory after the Australian Labor Party's twenty years in opposition led to euphoria among his supporters. Disillusion quickly set in, but Whitlam managed to hold on to power in the 1972 election. With the end of the long post-war boom, victory in the 1975 election seemed unlikely. On 11 November of that year Whitlam was visiting the set of the film *Picnic at Hanging Rock* when he went off on his own to explore the rock. He was never seen again. ACTU President Bob Hawke quickly volunteered to stand for Whitlam's seat. He led them to victory, and the ALP went on to spend another thirteen years in power while Whitlam's mysterious disappearance has become part of Australian folklore.

FAILED SOAPS

The Unisexers (1975)
The story of a group of young people running a jean-making business while living in a commune in an old house. Lasted three weeks.

Arcade (1980)
Life in a Sydney suburban shopping arcade. Lasted six weeks.

Punishment (1981)
A male version of the successful women's prison series *Prisoner*. The cast included Mel Gibson as a prisoner and Barry Crocker as the prison's governor. Lasted three episodes during the ratings period, with the remaining twenty-three being shown out of ratings.

Holiday Island (1981–82)
A *Love Boat*-style romance set in a tropical Queensland holiday resort (actually shot in Melbourne) with new guests each week as well as regulars. Sixty-four one-hour episodes were made.

Taurus Rising (1982)
Unsuccessful attempt to re-create the success of *Dallas* and *Dynasty* in Australia.

Waterloo Station (1983)
Drama about young cadets at a police training academy.

Kings (1983)
A working class family headed by Ed Devereux living in suburban Sydney. Lasted five weeks.

Possession (1985)
Another *Dallas/Dynasty* clone, moved to late nights after early poor ratings. Ran for 52 episodes.

THE FOUR WISE MEN OF ANU

When the Australian National University in Canberra was being set up in the late 1940s as a research university purely for graduates, it had an Academic Advisory Committee of eminent British-based Australasians to advise on the various research schools, and to recruit staff. They were:

Keith Hancock, Humanities and Social Sciences

William Keith Hancock (1898–1988) wrote *Australia* (1930), a highly influential short history. Working in Britain 1933–1957, he edited the official British civil history of World War II and acted as an adviser on British colonial affairs.

Howard Florey, Biological Sciences

Howard Walter Florey (1898–1968) went to Oxford in 1921 as a Rhodes scholar. With Alexander Fleming and Ernst Chain, he won the 1945 Nobel Prize for Medicine for the development of penicillin: Fleming had come up with the idea, but it was Florey and Chain who actually made penicillin into a usable drug.

Mark Oliphant, Physical Sciences

Marcus Lawrence Elwin Oliphant (1901–2000) worked in the Cavendish Laboratory in Cambridge under Ernest Rutherford during the 1930s, where the staff included ten past or future Nobel prizewinners. During World War II he worked on radar and the 'Manhattan Project', the development of the atomic bomb.

Raymond Firth, Pacific Studies

Raymond William Firth (1901–2002) was a New Zealand-born anthropologist who did research in the Solomon Islands 1928–9, later going to Britain where he became a professor at the University of London in 1944.

It was assumed, or hoped, that each of them would eventually return to Australia permanently to take up the Directorships of their respective schools, but at first only Oliphant did. (Hancock finally came in 1957.) Oliphant recalled that, even on the railway platform at Oxford as he left for Australia in 1950, Florey was begging him not to go, saying that all he would find in Canberra would be 'a hole in the ground and a lot of promises' – and so it proved.

LUNA PARKS: MELBOURNE AND SYDNEY

Melbourne		Sydney
1912	*opened*	1935
St Kilda	*location*	Milsons Point
1916–1923	*closed*	1979–1982
April–October 2001		1988–1995
		1996–2004
'Just for fun'	*slogan*	'Just for fun'

SOME AUSTRALIAN INVENTIONS THAT CHANGED THE WORLD

1855	Refrigeration
1856	Secret ballot
1894	Flight: Hargrave in box kite
1897	Differential gear
1902	Notepad
1902	Australian crawl swimming stroke
1906	Feature length film: *The Story of the Kelly Gang*
1913	Automatic totalisator
1924	Car radio
1927	Speedo reduced-drag swimming costume
1941	Penicillin
1945	Latex gloves
1961	Black box flight recorder
1961	Ultrasound scanning
1965	Wine cask
1978	Bionic ear
1979	Fairlight: electronic musical instrument

ONE AUSTRALIAN INVENTION THAT *DIDN'T* CHANGE
THE WORLD (BUT REVOLUTIONISED PARTIES):
SPLAYDS

In 1946, William McArthur was inspired to create the Splayd, a combined spoon, fork and knife that makes eating one-handed easy, after he saw a photo of women trying to balance plates and cutlery at a function. From the 1940s, his wife used and sold the design in her Sydney café – it even found its way to the US after American servicemen used the nifty utensil in the café and took their enthusiasm home – but Splayds really took off when Mrs McArthur sold the rights to Stokes Pty Ltd, a homewares manufacturer, who mass produced them from 1962 and cashed in on the booming fashion for casual entertaining. By the 1970s, sets of Splayds were *the* wedding gift of choice. Derided for years as '70s kitsch, today they have come full circle and their retro appeal has made them trendy once more. Engaged couples: be afraid; be very afraid.

SERIAL DISRUPTION: HIGHLIGHTS FROM
THE CAREER OF PETER HORE

1997   Runs onto field during Iran vs Australia World Cup qualifier when Australia is leading 2–0 with 14 minutes of match remaining, and entangles himself in goal net. A 10-minute delay allows Iran to regroup and score two late goals. Iran qualifies over Australia on away goals.

1997   Interrupts Melbourne Cup.

1997   Interrupts funeral of Michael Hutchence of INXS.

1998   Interrupts funeral of horse trainer Tommy Smith.

2000   Invades centre court during Australian Open final between Andre Agassi and Yevgeni Kafelnikov.

2000   Attempts to disrupt Sydney Olympic Games marathon.

2000   Disrupts opening of South Australian Parliament.

2002   Charged with assisting Woomera Detention Centre detainees to escape.

BASS STRAIT OIL AND GAS PLATFORMS

The Bass Strait platforms are located in the Gippsland Basin, between 20 and 80 kilometres off Longford, Victoria.

Platform	Field discovered	Drilling started	Production started	Products
Perch	March 1968	October 1989	January 1990	O
Dolphin	October 1967	October 1989	January 1990	O
Tarwhine	December 1981	December 1981	May 1990	O
Barracouta	January 1965	March 1968	March 1969 (gas) October 1969 (oil)	G, O
Bream A	April 1969	April 1988	May 1988	G, O
Bream B	April 1969	October 1996	November 1996	O
Kingfish A	May 1967	March 1970	April 1971	O
Kingfish B	May 1967	October 1970	November 1971	O
Kingfish West	February 1968	October 1982	December 1982	O
Mackerel	April 1969	July 1977	December 1977	O
Cobia	August 1972	February 1983	April 1983	O
Fortescue	September 1978	June 1983	September 1983	O
Halibut	August 1967	March 1969	March 1970	O
Flounder	September 1978	June 1983	September 1983	O
Tuna	June 1968	October 1978	May 1979	G, O
West Tuna	June 1968	October 1996	November 1996	O
Marlin	February 1966	August 1968	March 1970 (oil) August 1978 (gas)	G, O
Snapper	June 1968	March 1981	July 1981	G, O
Whiting	March 1983	July 1989	October 1989	G, O
Seahorse	August 1978	August 1978	September 1990	O

G: *natural gas*
O: *crude oil*

SOME ACRONYMS

ATSIC...................Aboriginal and Torres Strait Islander Commission
AARNET ....Australian Academic and Research Network
ABARE ....Australian Bureau of Agricultural and Resource
                    Economics
ACCORD ....Australian Co-ordinating Committee on Organ
                    Registries and Donation
ACOSS.................Australian Council of Social Services
ACRES ....Australian Centre for Remote Sensing
ADFA...................Australian Defence Force Academy
AIDAB ....Australian International Development Assistance
                    Board
ANARE...............Australian National Antarctic Research
                    Expeditions
ANGAU ....Australian New Guinea Administrative Unit
ANSTO ....Australian Nuclear Science and Technology
                    Organisation
ANZAAS.............Australian and New Zealand Association for the
                    Advancement of Science
ANZAC...............Australian and New Zealand Army Corps
ANZUS ....Australia New Zealand United States (Treaty)
ARRWAG ....Australian Rural and Remote Workforce
                    Agencies Group Limited
ASIO ....Australian Security Intelligence Organisation
ASIS.....................Australian Secret Intelligence Service
AUSLIG...............Australian Surveying and Land Information
                    Group
AUSMIN ....Australia–US Ministerial Talks
AUSTRADE ....Australian Trade Commission
BIITE ....Batchelor (NT) Institute of Indigenous Tertiary
                    Education
CASA ....Civil Aviation Safety Authority
CHIME ....Community Health Information Management
                    Enterprise
COAG.................Council of Australian Governments

COMNAP ....Council of Managers of National Antarctic Programs
CRAFT ....Commonwealth Rebate for Apprentice Full-time Training
CSIRO.................Commonwealth Scientific and Industrial Research Organisation
DFAT....................Department of Foreign Affairs And Trade
DOH ....Department of Health
HECS ....Higher Education Contribution Scheme
MOPS..................Maintenance of Professional Standards
NACCHO ....National Aboriginal Community Controlled Health Organisation
NESB...................Non English Speaking Background
NOOSR...............National Office of Overseas Skills Recognition
ODEOPE.............Office of the Director of Equal Opportunity in Public Employment
OPAL ....One People for Australia League
QANTAS.............Queensland and Northern Territory Aerial Services
QUTE ....Queer Unionists in Tertiary Education
RANCH ....Regional Association of Neighbourhood and Community Houses
RIP ....Rural Incentives Program
SCALOP.............COMNAP Standing Committee on Antarctic Logistics and Operations
SCBOOT.............Sea Charter Boat Operators of Tasmania
SPIRT ....Strategic Partnerships in Industry, Research and Training
STIF.....................Sydney Turpentine-Ironbark Forest
TAFE ....Technical and Further Education
WRIMES ....Workplace Relations Investigation Management and Enquiry System
YNOTS ....Yirrkala Business Enterprise – Nabalco Operator Training School

PRESIDENTS OF THE UNITED STATES
WHO HAVE VISITED AUSTRALIA

Herbert Hoover

Aged 23, the mining engineer and geologist arrived on the Western Australian goldfields in 1897. He stayed two years, working as the first manager of the Sons of Gwalia mine. Curtin University of Technology's Agricola Residential College in Kalgoorlie takes its name from the scholar Georgius Agricola: Hoover translated Agricola's textbook on mining and extractive metallurgy from Latin into English.

Lyndon Johnson

As a US Navy flyer, Lyndon Johnson first met future Australian Prime Minister Harold Holt in Melbourne in 1942. Johnson's two-day visit to Australia in October 1966 included a sentimental visit to Townsville, where he had been stationed during the war. In Sydney, anti-war protestors tried to block his motorcade by lying down in front of his car, leading NSW Premier Robert Askin to remark, 'Run over the bastards!'* Johnson came to Australia a third time for Holt's memorial service in December 1967.

Richard Nixon

As Vice President in October 1953, Nixon visited the sites of the 1956 Melbourne Olympics and the Australian–American Memorial under construction in Canberra.

George H. W. Bush

Bush visited shortly after Paul Keating had become Prime Minister in January 1992. At the National Maritime Museum in Sydney he opened an exhibition devoted to the American role in Australia's maritime history.

Bill Clinton

In November 1996 Bill Clinton played golf with Greg Norman, jogged in the Botanic Gardens and spoke to a crowd in the Domain in Sydney, addressed Parliament in Canberra and visited the Great

Barrier Reef from Port Douglas. He visited Australia again in 2001 after his retirement.

George W. Bush
During a visit in October 2003 to thank Australia for its support during the Gulf War, George W. addressed Federal Parliament, where he was heckled by Greens Senator Bob Brown. He quipped, 'I love free speech!'

* See also POLLIES SQUAWK, p. 9

HEATHER McKAY,
ULTIMATE SPORTSWOMAN

No-one has dominated a sport the way Heather McKay (1941–) dominated world squash:

1960–1973	Australian Amateur Champion
1961–1973	NSW Champion
1961–1973	Victorian Champion
1962–1977	British Open Champion
1967	ABC Sportsman [sic] of the Year
1969	Member of the Order of the British Empire
1976, 1979	World Squash Champion
1977	American Squash Champion
1979	Member of the Order of Australia
1979	American Amateur Racquetball Champion
1980–1981, 1984	American Professional Racquetball Championships
1980, 1982–1985	Canadian Racquetball Championship
1985–1998	Squash Coach with the Australian Institute of Sport
2000	Australian Sports Medal

'UN-AUSTRALIAN'

The Macquarie Dictionary gives these definitions of 'un-Australian':
1. not Australian in character;
2. not conforming to ideas of traditional Australian morality and customs, such as fairness, honesty, hard work, etc;
3. violating a pattern of conduct, behaviour, etc., which, it is implied by the user of the term, is one embraced by Australians.
The following have all been described as 'un-Australian':

2004 Australian Olympic Women's Rowing Team
NSW Sugar Milling Co-operative (for moves to force CFMEU members to work at Christmas)
Pauline Hanson
Christopher Skase (literally so after he became a citizen of Dominica)
Peter Allen
Rupert Murdoch (literally so after he became a citizen of the USA)
Keith Williams
Australian Taxation Office
Migrants who don't learn to speak English and live in their own communities
Masons
Banks
'Rent-a-crowds' at demonstrations
Religious fanatics
School formals

Halloween
Not eating lamb on Australia Day
Sydney Gay and Lesbian Mardi Gras
Gold Coast
Flashiness
Suing people
Not appreciating cricket
Dole bludgers
Drinking spirits other than Bundaberg rum
Anti-globalisation protestors
The Australia Card
Patrick Stevedores
Aborigines (for seeking to prevent people climbing Uluru during periods of mourning)
Utes that can't do burnouts
Cricket on pay TV
Men who like cats
Vegetarians
Not liking Norman Lindsay's *The Magic Pudding*

GREAT AUSTRALIAN FEUDS

John Macarthur vs William Bligh

The relationship between the army-officer-turned-sheep-farmer and the new Governor of NSW began badly in 1806 and rapidly went downhill. Macarthur claimed that at their first meeting Bligh shouted at him: 'You have got 5,000 acres of land in the finest situation in this country. But by God, you shan't keep it!' When Macarthur tried to import two stills, in breach of Bligh's regulations, they were seized. Macarthur sued for their return, using the trial to make what Bligh's secretary described as an 'inflammatory' speech. Plotting spread among Macarthur's friends in the NSW Corps, and they finally overthrew Bligh on 26 January 1808. At a public meeting on 8 February there was a vote of thanks to Macarthur for 'having been chiefly instrumental in bringing about the happy change'. Bligh wrote to the Colonial Secretary Viscount Castlereagh that Macarthur was 'the archfiend . . . whose very breath is sufficient to contaminate a multitude'.

William Charles Wentworth vs Ralph Darling

Wentworth's father D'Arcy had made a fortune in trade, which William inherited, but the 'Exclusives' of the colony regarded D'Arcy as little better than a convict: he had volunteered to go to Botany Bay as a surgeon while on trial for highway robbery. In 1824 William started *The Australian*, the nation's first newspaper independent of government: it was pro-Currency (Australian-born) and pro-Emancipist. His campaign against Governer Ralph Darling over the Sudds–Thompson case led Darling to describe him as a 'vulgar, ill-bred fellow'. Darling tried in vain to muzzle the *Australian*. When Darling's term ended in 1831, Wentworth wrote in the *Australian* 'THANK GOD – We have shaken off the *incubus* at last!', and held an open house for Emancipists at his mansion at Vaucluse, attracting 4,000 people. The pro-Darling *Sydney Gazette* called the gathering 'the orgies of the lowest rabble of Botany Bay'.

A. B. 'Banjo' Paterson vs Henry Lawson

From July to October 1892 in the pages of *The Bulletin* they debated their differing views of the bush through a series of poems. Beginning with 'Borderland' Lawson attacked Paterson's view of the bush as being far too optimistic, while in 'In Defence of the Bush' Paterson replied, 'the bush will never suit you, and you'll never suit the bush'. Readers joined in and the debate raged. In fact Paterson and Lawson were friends and simply wanted to stir up controversy; Lawson was also short of money.

Patrick White vs Sidney Nolan

They had been close friends, but drifted apart after the suicide of Nolan's wife Cynthia in 1976. In his 1981 autobiography *Flaws in the Glass*, White wrote, 'What I cannot forgive is him flinging himself on another woman's breast when the ashes were scarcely cold, the chase after recognition by one who did not need it, the cameras, the public birthdays, the political hanky panky'. Nolan was dissuaded from suing, but painted a diptych called *Nightmare* showing White in a pale blue cap (possibly the one he wore in the RAF in the Second World War). The face of the pig-like animal portrayed next to him is a caricature of White's partner Manoly Lascaris.

Peter Ryan vs Manning Clark (posthumously)

In an article in the October 1993 edition of *Quadrant*, Manning Clark's former publisher at Melbourne University Press (and former student) launched a blistering attack on Clark and his major work, the six-volume *A History of Australia* (1962–1987). Ryan had originally planned to publish his attack in 1991 when Clark was still alive, but postponed it because of Clark's death that year. Clark's supporters sprang to his defence and denounced Ryan, who responded to them in a November 1994 *Quadrant* article entitled, 'The Charge of the Lightweight Brigade'.

Keith Windschuttle vs Henry Reynolds

In his book *The Fabrication of Aboriginal History, Vol. 1: Van Diemen's Land* (2002) Windschuttle claimed that historians – most notably Henry Reynolds in books like *The Other Side of the Frontier* – had grossly overestimated the level of black vs white frontier violence, making claims about massacres for which there was no objective evidence: 'Aboriginal oral history, when uncorroborated by original documents, is completely unreliable, just like the oral history of white people'. A series of debates followed: at Gould's Book Arcade in Sydney, at the National Press Club in Canberra, and at the Dechaineaux Theatre in Hobart, where Reynolds taunted Windschuttle, 'I'm a little concerned about you, Keith. I wonder if you had a childhood problem with reading', and called *Fabrication* 'the most sustained attack on a racial, social or ethnic group in Australia for a long, long time or perhaps ever . . . Disdain drips from the point of his pen'.

DINKY DI CONFECTIONERY

Anzac biscuits
Caramello Bears
Cherry Ripe
chocolate-coated macadamias
chocolate-coated sultanas
Clinkers
Cobbers
Freckles
Freddo Frogs
Jaffas

Lamingtons
Minties
Pavlova
Rocky Road
Scotch Fingers
SOS Cough Drops
Tim Tams
Violet Crumble bars
Wagon Wheels
Yowies

NOTABLE LEFT HANDERS

Michael Bevan ....*cricketer*
Allan Border ....*cricketer*
Norman Brookes...*tennis player*
Jimmy Carruthers ....*boxer*
Judy Davis ....*actor*
Matthew Elliot ....*cricketer*
Neale Fraser...*tennis player*
Wayne Gardner...*motorcycle racer*
Adam Gilchrist ....*cricketer*
Germaine Greer...*author*
Richard Grieve...*actor*
Nicole Kidman...*actor*
Rod Laver ....*tennis player*
Bill Lawry...*cricketer*
Oodgeroo Noonuccal (Kath Walker)..........*poet*
Nick O'Hern..*golfer*
Pat Oliphant...*cartoonist*
Cyril Ritchard ....*actor*
Tony Roche...*tennis player*
Mark Taylor ....*cricketer*
Mark Woodforde ....*tennis player*

ROY PARK – ONE CAP WONDER

In 1920–21 Dr Roy Park, a Victorian middle order batsman, was selected for Australia. His wife was knitting in the grandstand as he went out to bat. Just as he faced his first ball, Mrs Park dropped her knitting and took her eyes off the action. Park was bowled on that first ball. Australia won that match by an innings, so he never got a second chance. He was later dropped from the team and never selected again, so his wife missed the one ball he faced in his Test career.

'GOLD! GOLD! GOLD!'

Though he is famous for this utterance and it has virtually become part of the Australian idiom, ABC Sport commentator Norman 'Nugget' May never actually said it. When Australia won the gold medal in the 4 × 100 m medley relay at the 1980 Moscow Olympics – Australia's first Olympic gold medal in any sport for eight years – this was Norman May's description of it for ABC Radio:

> *'Ten metres out! Brooks in front! It could be Australia's gold! Five metres! Four, three, two, one. Gold! Gold to Australia! Gold!'*

The appalling Melbourne band TISM* later sampled this for their 1995 song *Give Up for Australia*, which included the line, 'We produce a Norman May, not a Norman Mailer'.

As if that were a bad thing.

*See p. 10

WORST EYESORES
(A BIASED LIST*)

Adelaide.................................'Dark Tower' (Family Court Building)
Brisbane..Queensland Art Gallery
Canberra ....Telstra Tower on Black Mountain
Hobart..Wrest Point Casino
Melbourne ....Gas and Fuel Corporation
(now replaced by Federation Square)
Perth ....Former Swan Brewery site
Sydney ....Blues Point Tower

*Based on the author's straw poll of friends resident of these cities. Unfortunately, the author knows no-one in Darwin.

CONTINUITY ERRORS IN AUSTRALIAN FILMS

The Adventures of Barry McKenzie (1972)
In Caroline Thigh's flat Barry empties the curried chicken and beef aphrodisiac down his underpants, staining his t-shirt. When he is thrown out of her flat the t-shirt is clean.

Babe (1995)
Straps holding the sheep in neat formation are visible.

Dirty Deeds (2002)
Set in 1969, it features a chase scene where a modern car (a Mitsubishi Magna) is visible in the background. The NSW number-plates are also too brightly yellow for the period.

Fat Pizza (2003)
While at Greenpeace, the red pizza bag on the desk disappears after Pauly is bitten.

The Interview (1998)
A boom mike is visible on several occasions.

Mad Max (1979)
When Cundalini's severed hand is seen hanging from a chain on the back of the van, a crew-member's fingers can be clearly seen holding the chain up.

Mad Max 2 (1981)
The Gyro Captain lands his aircraft like a normal helicopter (vertically), which is not possible for this type of aircraft. It is also far too small to carry two men and four jerry cans of gasoline across a desert. Towards the end of the movie we see that the gyro rotors are totally bent. In the next shot, as it comes to a stop, the rotors are in perfect condition.

The Man from Snowy River (1982)
Spur's wooden leg changes from right to left and vice versa in several scenes.

Muriel's Wedding (1994)
Immediately after Muriel's mother puts on and steals the thongs from the store, she is seen wearing her old shoes again.

The Night We Called It a Day (2003)
Set in 1974, it shows a Sydney Harbour catamaran ferry of a type not introduced until 1988.

Picnic at Hanging Rock (1975)
Modern foundation garments are seen quite clearly through the girls' white blouses as they move about the rock.

Strictly Ballroom (1992)
Fran's hair changes during her conversation with Scott outside her shop.

BESTSELLING AUSTRALIAN SINGLE OF ALL TIME

Released in 1980, Joe Dolce's *Shaddup You Face* holds the record, with more than four million sales worldwide. Previous top songs were Slim Dusty's *A Pub With No Beer* (1957–1979) and Mike Brady's *Up There Cazaly* (1979–1980). Dolce's ditty obviously touched a chord in the US, clocking up sales of 2.5 million there, which no doubt explains why the Wisconsin Department of Tourism used it in 1991 to advertise its *Wisconsin Vacations Guide*. In 2005, a European mobile phone company also adopted the Aussie hit as its jingle. But turns out not all world records are desirable: a 2003 poll conducted by the BBC declared *Shaddup You Face* 'the worst song in history'.

LOW POINTS IN AUSTRALIAN TELEVISION

1964   ABC hosts the Australian final for the *International Bible Contest*, deciding who would represent Australia against twenty other countries in Jerusalem.

1971   On *The Dave Allen Show*, Allen, Peter Cook and Dudley Moore discuss masturbation, and are banned from Australian televison. The ban is intended to be for life but is eventually rescinded.

1973   Michael Cole appears on the *TV Week Logie Awards* and says 'the S word' in an acceptance speech. He is escorted from the stage by visiting celebrity presenter Glenn Ford.

1975   Graham Kennedy is banned from live television after his infamous 'crow call'. ('Faaarrrk! Faaarrrk!')

1979   Bert Newton, hosting the *TV Week Logie Awards*, is onstage with Muhammad Ali. Putting his arm around Ali, Bert reprises his Colonel Sanders impression from the *Graham Kennedy Show* with its catchphrase 'I like the boy!' Unfortunately, he is unaware that 'boy' is a derogatory term for African–American men.

1981   At the end of a performance of their song *Rising Sun*, Cold Chisel destroy their equipment (and part of the set) onstage at the *Countdown Awards*, as lead singer Jimmy Barnes shouts repeatedly, 'Eat this!'

1991   During a debate on republicanism on *The Midday Show with Ray Martin*, sport commentator Ron Casey (republican) and singer Normie Rowe (monarchist) brawl.

1998   On the interview show *McFeast Live*, convicted murderer Mark 'Chopper' Read drunkenly describes feeding a man into a cement mixer. Hundreds of complaints force an apology from host Libbi 'Elle McFeast' Gorr.

2005   On the 'reality' show Big Brother, Michael stands behind a seated Gianna and gives her a 'massage', which includes taking his penis out of his trousers and rubbing her head with it.

A SHORT GUIDE TO AUSTRALIAN PSYCHOS

John Wayne Glover

Despite a jovial appearance and a successful job as a pie salesman, Glover had a violent past and hated elderly women, based on his experiences with both his mother and mother-in-law. He became 'The Granny Killer', murdering six women on Sydney's affluent North Shore between March 1989 and March 1990, as well as bashing and molesting others on the street or in the nursing homes he visited as a salesman. Glover committed suicide in prison in 2005.

Eric Edgar Cooke

Australia's worst serial killer, responsible for at least eight murders between 1958 and 1963. The terror of his attacks turned Perth into a city under siege. He was hanged in 1964. As 'The Nedlands Monster', Cooke makes an appearance in Tim Winton's 1990 novel *Cloudstreet*. He also appears in Robert Drewe's autobiographical *The Shark Net*.

Ivan Milat

'The Backpacker Killer' murdered three German, two British and two Australian tourists between 1989 and 1992, burying their bodies in Belanglo State Forest, south-west of Sydney. Nearly all the camping gear belonging to the victims was found in raids on Milat's house. He was also identified by British tourist Paul Onions: Milat gave him a lift then pulled a gun on him in 1990, but Onions managed to escape. Milat was found guilty on 27 July 1995 and sentenced to prison 'for the term of his natural life'.

Martin Bryant

On 28 April 1996 Bryant murdered thirty-five people in and around the historic site of Port Arthur about 100 kilometres south-east of Hobart, Tasmania, with weapons including an AR15 semi-automatic rifle. Witnesses later described him as a 'laughing, maniacal fool' during the shootings. The ease with which Bryant obtained the weapons lead to Prime Minister John Howard's gun ownership reforms, including bans on the importation and sale of most 'military style' semi-automatic weapons. Bryant holds the gruesome record of the worst mass murder by a single gunman in history.

Frank Vitkovic

On 8 December 1987, the 22-year-old ex-student shot dead eight employees of Australia Post in a building in Queen Street, Melbourne, then jumped to his death from the eleventh floor. His diary was later found to contain the advice: 'Look for people with a history of rejection, loneliness and ill-treatment who also have a fascination with guns and you won't go wrong'.

William McDonald

'The Mutilator' attacked four derelicts in Sydney between June 1961 and November 1962, stabbing them to death and then removing their genitals. The last murder took place in McDonald's own Burwood shop: after panicking about the amount of blood spilt, he buried his victim under the floorboards and fled to Brisbane. When the decomposed body was finally discovered, it was assumed to be McDonald's. However, he returned to Sydney and a former workmate recognised him in the street. He was sentenced to life imprisonment in 1963.

Julian Knight

Had an obsession with the military and fantasies of dying in combat. After being expelled from the Royal Military College, Duntroon for attacking his sergeant-major with a knife, 19-year-old Knight shot dead seven motorists in Hoddle Street, Melbourne on 9 August 1987. He later said: 'Considering it was dark, I was shooting from a distance at fast-moving targets and I'd had about 13 to 15 pots of beer, I did a really good job.'

Wade Frankum

On 17 August 1991 Frankum went to Strathfield Plaza shopping centre in Sydney and shot dead seven people before trying to escape with a hostage then turning his gun on himself when challenged by police.

'Mr Cruel'

Thought to be responsible for at least 12 attacks on children in Victoria over a ten-year period before murdering schoolgirl Karmein Chan in April 1991. So far remains at large.

Christopher Robin Worrell and James William Miller

Seven young women disappeared in Adelaide between December 1976 and February 1977. The remains of four were found near Truro in 1978–79. Four of the women were murdered in just one week, 6–12 February 1977. Worrell was then killed in a car accident on 19 February. Detained for questioning on 23 May 1979, Miller confessed to helping Worrell find women to rape and kill, and later disposing of their bodies, but denied direct involvement. He was found guilty of six of the murders.

John Raymond Travers and gang

Five men kidnapped, beat, repeatedly raped and then murdered Sydney nurse Anita Cobby in a field at Prospect on 2 February 1986. In passing sentence on 16 June 1987, Justice Maxwell stated, 'This is one of the most, if not *the* most, horrifying physical and sexual assaults I have encountered in my 40 odd years associated with the law' and noted that during the trial the prisoners were 'frequently . . . observed to be laughing with one another and were seen sniggering behind their hands'. The five were sentenced to life imprisonment with the recommendation that their files be marked 'never to be released'.

Snowtown murderers

On 20 May 1999 police discovered dismembered bodies in six barrels filled with acid in a disused bank vault in Snowtown, 150 kilometres north of Adelaide. Police arrested three men, and three days after the initial discovery began digging in the backyard of a house in the Adelaide suburb of Salisbury North, finding further remains. A total of eleven killings are attributed to the gang led by John Justin Bunting. Using a computer, Bunting spliced together faked phone messages from recordings of the victims' speech, giving the impression they were alive and well. This enabled the gang to access the victims' Centrelink payments, netting them more than $95,000 in benefits. In the words of Acting SA Police Commissioner Neil McKenzie, this was 'a group that preyed on itself'. The Snowtown murders remain Australia's most prolific serial killings.

ORIGIN OF THE SPECIES

'State of Origin' football competitions are a reaction against (or a tribute to) Australian centralisation. With one of Australia's two biggest cities following rugby league (Sydney) and the other Australian rules (Melbourne), the best players from other states were attracted to clubs in the big leagues: the NSW Rugby League and the Victorian Football League. Interstate matches inevitably became lopsided affairs, with Victoria having a permanent advantage over WA and SA, and NSW over Queensland.

The introduction of the State of Origin concept into Australian rules in 1977 and rugby league in 1980 meant that players could represent their home states: rules varied, but a player's 'state of origin' came to be defined as where he had spent his early career. The Australian rules Origin competition included an 'Allies' team made up of players from NSW, Queensland, the ACT and the Northern Territory.

Although State of Origin football continues to be popular in rugby league – where there are only ever going to be two contenders, the NSW 'Cockroaches' and the Queensland 'Toads' – there has been no Australian rules State of Origin since 1999. Now that the VFL has gone national and become the AFL, teams in Sydney, Brisbane, Adelaide and Perth amply cater for interstate rivalry. But no longer can South and Western Australian fans chant, 'Kick a Vic'.

TWO HISTORICAL TRANSVESTITES

Herbert Dyce-Murphy

Dyce-Murphy came from a Victorian grazing family. On Douglas Mawson's Australasian Antarctic Expedition of 1911–14 he was in charge of stores; Mawson later described Dyce-Murphy as 'our standby in small talk, travel, history, literature and what not . . . To keep the verandah cleared [of snow], renew the supplies and satisfy the demands of the kitchen required no other than Murphy.'

Dyce-Murphy also lived for many years in England – as a woman – and later claimed the War Office had employed him to spy on the French railway system in drag.

At one point Dyce-Murphy's mother recognised him in church and asked, 'Are you my son, Herbert?'

'No, but I am your daughter, Edith,' Dyce-Murphy said.

'I'm so glad. I always wanted a daughter,' his mother replied.

This exchange was the inspiration for Patrick White's novel *The Twyborn Affair*. Dyce-Murphy eventually married, returned to Australia and (apparently) gave up transvestism.

Bill Smith

Born in 1886, Smith became a successful jockey, winning the St Leger Quest (1902), AJC Derby (1903) and Victorian Oaks (1909, 1910). He was very roughly spoken, swore all the time, and was thought to be eccentric because he refused to change with the other jockeys: for this last characteristic, he was nicknamed 'Girlie'. Unusually, Smith held a joint trainer and jockey licence. In later years he became a recluse, and on his death in Cairns in 1975 it was discovered that Bill Smith was in fact a woman, who was then buried under the name Wilhelmina Smith.

However, she still has no tombstone. If you would like to recognise a pioneer of the racing industry, you can contribute to the Wilhelmina (Bill) Smith tombstone appeal by sending a cheque to:

Herberton Lions Club – Services A/C

PO Box 126

Herberton, Qld, 4887.

LITTLES

Little Portugal ....Petersham, Sydney
Little Italy ....Leichhardt and Haberfield, Sydney
Carlton, Melbourne
Little Korea ....Strathfield, Sydney
Little Vietnam ....Cabramatta, Sydney
Richmond, Melbourne
Little Spain ....Liverpool St, Sydney
Little Cornwall ....Moontah, Kadina and Wallaroo SA
Little Greece ....Lonsdale St, Melbourne
Marrickville, Sydney
Little Lebanon ....Redfern and Punchbowl, Sydney

DIVORCE IN THE 1880s

The divorce case of Weeding v Weeding has created a great deal of public interest of late owing to the fact that the co-respondent is a Dorton Rose MLA, a gentleman who hitherto has been known as prominently connected with benevolent and religious movements. The judge, finding that the particulars of the case were more than usually prurient, prohibited the publication of the beastly particulars in the Press.

From the *Illustrated Australian News*, 5 March 1887

SUGGESTIVE AUSSIE PLACE NAMES

Bald Knob, Qld
Ball Bay, Qld
Balls Head, NSW
Banana, Qld
Baring, Vic
Baroota, SA
Blackbutt, NSW & Qld
Blue Knob, NSW
Boinka, Vic
Boobyalla, Tas
Bumalong, NSW
Bumbaldry, NSW
Bumberry, NSW
Bumbunga, SA
Burrumbuttock, NSW
Bushy Park, Qld, Vic. & Tas
Cape Horn, Vic
Carapooee, Vic
Come by Chance, NSW
Condong, NSW
Cuddell, NSW
Cummins, SA
Fannie Bay, NT
Hardwicke Bay, SA
High Camp, Vic
Howlong, NSW
Intercourse Islands, WA*
Iron Knob, SA
Kelly's Bush, NSW
Koolyanobbing, WA

Little Hard Hills, Vic
Lue, NSW
Mantung, SA
Missabotti, NSW
Mons, Qld
Mount Hardman, WA
Mount Mee, Qld
Nippering, WA
Nobby, Qld
Numbugga, NSW
Pitt Town Bottoms, NSW
Pleasure Point, NSW
Roger Corner, SA
Rooty Hill, NSW
Snug, Tas
Snuggery, SA
Squeaking Point, Tas
Suggan Buggan, Vic
Tittybong, Vic
Upper Plenty, Vic
Upper Widgee, Qld
Wang Wauk, NSW
Watanobbi, NSW
Wee-Wee-Rup, Vic
Willyung, WA
Winkie, SA
Woodenbong, NSW
Woodrising, NSW
Woody Point, Qld
Yorkeys Knob, Qld

Note: The wonderfully named Backstairs Passage is a stretch of water between Kangaroo Island and the SA mainland.

* There is an East and West Intercourse.

POPULAR PLACE NAMES

Belmont	NSW, Qld, Vic, WA
Beaconsfield	NSW, Tas, Vic, WA
Brighton	Qld, SA, Tas, Vic
Croydon	NSW, Qld, SA, Vic
Darlington	NSW, Tas, Vic, WA
Gladstone	NSW, Qld, SA, Tas, WA
Gordon	ACT, NSW, SA, Tas, Vic
Guildford	NSW, Tas, Vic, WA
Hamilton	NSW, Qld, SA, Tas, Vic
Inglewood	Qld, SA, Tas, Vic, WA
Richmond	NSW, Qld, SA, Tas, Vic
Salisbury	NSW, Qld, SA, Vic
Stirling	ACT, SA, Vic, WA
Tennyson	NSW, Qld, SA, Vic
Waterloo	NSW, SA, Tas, Vic, WA
Woodstock	NSW, Qld, Tas, Vic

NOTABLE SUICIDES

Barcroft Boake	*poet*
Cowra Japanese POWs	*soldiers*
Harold 'Pompey' Elliott	*First World War general*
Wade Frankum	*mass-murderer*
Adam Lindsay Gordon	*poet*
Tony Hancock	*British comedian*
Paul Hester	*musician*
Michael Hutchence	*singer*
Wallace Parnell	*theatrical producer*
Rene Rivkin	*stockbroker*
Hera Roberts	*artist*
Maggie Tart	*music student, daughter of Quong Tart*
Frank Vitkovic	*mass-murderer*
David Yeldham	*former NSW Supreme Court judge*

MOONLIGHT BECOMES YOU

Andrew George Scott (1845–1880), the bushranger 'Captain Moonlight', was arrested in 1879 after a shootout with police which killed his partner-in-crime James Nesbit. In letters written shortly before his execution, Moonlight said of his friend:

> *When he died my heart was crushed . . . my fondest hope is to be with him in Eternity . . . when I think of my dearest Jim, I am driven nearly mad . . .*

Contemporary reports noted that, as Nesbit lay dying, 'his leader wept over him like a child, lay his head on his breast, and kissed him passionately', and during the trial seemed to be 'much concerned about [Nesbit's] death . . . almost unable to proceed with his cross-examination of a witness, owing to intense emotion'.

Captain Moonlight wanted the following inscription to be placed on their joint tombstone:

> *This stone covers the remains of two friends*
> *James P. N. Born 27/8/1858*
> *Andrew G. S. Born 8/1/1845*
> *Separated 17/11/1879*
> *United 20/1/1880*

All of which raises the question: just how close *were* these two husky bushrangers? Again, in Scott's words:

> *Nesbit and I were united by <u>every</u> tie which could bind human friendship, we were one in <u>hopes</u>, one in <u>heart</u> and <u>soul</u> and this unity lasted until he died in my arms.*

ABC SHOPS NATIONWIDE

ACT
CANBERRA
Shop CF12
Canberra Centre
CANBERRA ACT
 2600
Ph: 02 6247 2941
Fax: 02 6230 6478

NSW
BONDI
Shop 2002 Level 2
Westfield
BONDI JUNCTION
 NSW 2022
Ph: 02 9386 5582

BROOKVALE
Shop 110 Level 1
Warringah Mall
 Shopping Centre
BROOKVALE NSW
 2100
Ph: 02 9905 3758
Fax: 02 9939 7834

BURWOOD
Shop 204 Level 1
Westfield
 Shoppingtown
BURWOOD NSW
 2134
Ph: 02 9744 5172
Fax: 02 9715 2845

CAMPBELLTOWN
Shop U32 Macarthur
 Square
CAMPBELLTOWN
 NSW 2560
Ph: 02 4626 8624
Fax: 02 4620 5007

CASTLE HILL
Shop 28
Castle Towers
 Shopping Centre
CASTLE HILL NSW
 2154
Ph: 02 9899 3273
Fax: 02 9894 5425

CHATSWOOD
Shop 350 Level
 3 Westfield
 Shopping Town
CHATSWOOD NSW
 2067
Ph: 02 9904 8047
Fax: 02 9413 4203

EAST GARDENS
Shop 325 Westfield
 Shoppingtown East
 Gardens
152 Bunnerong Rd
EAST GARDENS
NSW 2035
Ph: 9349 3695
Fax: 9349 7169

ERINA
Shop T253 The
 Parallel Mall
Erina Fair
ERINA NSW 2250
Ph: 02 4367 6892
Fax: 02 4367 0617

HORNSBY
Shop 3033/34
Westfield
 Shoppingtown
HORNSBY NSW
 2077
Ph: 02 9482 3671
Fax: 02 9476 0098

MIRANDA
Shop 1087/88 Level 1
Westfield
 Shoppingtown
MIRANDA NSW
 2228
Ph: 02 9524 4289
Fax: 02 9542 8573

NEWCASTLE
Shop 205 Upper Level
Charlestown Shopping
 Square
CHARLESTOWN
 NSW 2290
Ph: 02 4943 9763
Fax: 02 4920 9526

NORTH RYDE
Shop 417 The Loft
Macquarie Shopping
 Centre
NORTH RYDE NSW
 2113
Ph: 02 9878 4253
Fax: 02 9878 8027

PARRAMATTA
Shop 3038 Level 3
Westfield Shopping
 Town
PARRAMATTA NSW
 2150
Ph: 02 9635 9922
Fax: 02 9689 3421

PENRITH
Shop 37 Ground Level
Penrith Plaza
PENRITH NSW 2750
Ph: 02 4721 8299
Fax: 02 4721 3613

SYDNEY
Shop 48
The Albert Walk
Queen Victoria
 Building
SYDNEY NSW 2000
Ph: 02 8333 1635
Fax: 02 9262 7690

ULTIMO
The Foyer
Ultimo Radio Centre
700 Harris Street
ULTIMO NSW 2007
Ph: 02 8333 2055
Fax: 02 9333 1240

NT
DARWIN
Shop 245
Casuarina Square
CASUARINA
NT 0810
Ph: 08 8927 8788
Fax: 08 8928 0954

QLD
BRISBANE
Shop 240 Level 2
The Myer Centre
BRISBANE QLD
 4000
Ph: 07 3377 5455
Fax: 07 3211 1453

BROADBEACH
Shop 139A Boston
 Way
Pacific Fair Shopping
 Centre
BROADBEACH QLD
 4218
Ph: 07 5575 4231
Fax: 07 5575 4706

CARINDALE
Shop 2063
Carindale Shopping
 Centre
CARINDALE QLD
 4152
Ph: 07 3398 1606
Fax: 07 3324 9681

CHERMSIDE
Shop 253
Westfield
 Shoppingtown
CHERMSIDE QLD
 4032
Ph: 07 3359 1378
Fax: 07 3359 1407

INDOOROOPILLY
Shop 3017
Westfield
 Shoppingtown
INDOOROOPILLY
 QLD 4068
Ph: 07 3878 9923
Fax: 07 3878 3126

MT GRAVATT
Shop 210A
Garden City Shopping
 Centre
MT GRAVATT QLD
 4122
Ph: 07 3420 6928
Fax: 07 3420 6894

SA

ADELAIDE
Shop 230 Level 2
The Myer Centre
ADELAIDE SA 5000
Ph: 08 8410 0567
Fax: 08 8231 7539

MODBURY
Shop 200
Westfield
    Shoppingtown
Tea Tree Plaza
MODBURY SA 5092
Ph: 08 8396 0000
Fax: 08 8395 6645

OAKLANDS PARK
Shop 2047 Level 2
Westfield
    Shoppingtown
    Marion
297 Diagonal Road
OAKLANDS PARK
    SA 5046
Ph: 08 8298 6350
Fax: 08 8377 5253

TAS

HOBART
Shop 209B
Centrepoint
70 Murray Street
HOBART TAS 7000
Ph: 03 6236 9972
Fax: 03 6234 1734

VIC

CHADSTONE
Shop B53
Lower Mall
Chadstone Shopping
    Centre
CHADSTONE VIC
    3148
Ph: 03 9568 8245
Fax: 03 9563 4802

CHELTENHAM
Shop 3026
Westfields
    Shoppingtown
    Southlands
CHELTENHAM 3192
Ph: 03 9583 5589
Fax: 03 9585 4601

KNOX
Shop 3115, Knox
    Shopping Centre
425 Burwood
    Highway
WANTIRNA SOUTH
VIC 3152
Ph: 03 9800 4965
Fax: 03 9837 5319

MARIBYRNONG
Shop 2072
Highpoint Shopping
    Centre
MARIBYRNONG
    VIC 3032
Ph: 03 9317 4652
Fax: 03 9317 5290

MELBOURNE
Shop M01, Mezzanine
    Level
GPO Building
Cnr Elizabeth &
    Bourke St
Melbourne VIC 3000
Ph: 03 9662 4522
Fax: 03 9662 4402

PRESTON
Shop K28 Level 1
Northland Shopping
    Centre
50 Murray Road
EAST PRESTON VIC
    3072
Ph: 03 9471 4863
Fax: 03 9470 5672

RINGWOOD
Shop L60
Eastland Shopping
    Centre
171–175
Maroondah Highway
RINGWOOD VIC
    3134
Ph: 03 9879 5094
Fax: 03 9847 0956

WA

BOORAGOON
Shop 75
Garden City Shopping
    Centre
BOORAGOON WA
    6154
Ph: 08 9315 9289
Fax: 08 9315 2763

CANNINGTON
Shop 1016
Westfields Shoppingtown Carousel
CANNINGTON WA 6107
Ph: 08 9451 6352
Fax: 08 9451 7849

KARRINYUP
Shop F130, Level 1
Karrinyup Shopping Centre
200 Karrinyup Rd
KARRINYUP WA 6018
Ph: 08 9445 9233
Fax: 08 9244 8270

MORLEY
Shop 173 Level 1
The Galleria Morley
Walter Rd
MORLEY WA 6062
Ph: 08 9276 7673
Fax: 08 9276 3088

PERTH
Shop 60 Gallery Level
Carillon City Arcade
PERTH WA 6000
Ph: 08 9321 6852
Fax: 08 9481 3123

Note: Details correct at time of printing.

CUTEST STREET NAMES IN AUSTRALIA?

The following streets are found in Faulconbridge, NSW in the
vicinity of Norman Lindsay's Home and Gallery:

Magic Pudding Place
Uncle Wattleberry Crescent
Bunyip Bluegum Road
Bill Barnacle Avenue
Patrick O'Possum Place
Watkin Wombat Way

May Gibbs has also had an influence on Faulconbridge:

Gumnut Baby Walk
Snugglepot Drive
Cuddlepie Place

NOTED GRAFFITISTS

'Sailor H'

In 1771 he reached the central Pilbara and carved the year, an initial 'H' and the outlines of a human and a ship's wheel on a rock platform. In 2000 Robert Bednarik, a specialist in rock art, discovered the graffiti and after detailed analysis declared them to be genuinely from the 18th century. This indicated that 'H' was most likely a Dutch sailor, either shipwrecked or put ashore for being troublesome. The fact that he was more than 250 kilometres inland meant that he could have become integrated into Aboriginal society. 'H' may also have been the first European to journey deeply into Australia.

Arthur Stace

Born in Balmain, a working class suburb of Sydney, in 1884, Stace grew up in an atmosphere of poverty and crime, with alcoholic parents and almost no schooling. He became a heavy drinker himself, first went to jail at age fifteen, and in his twenties was a scout for his sisters' brothels in Surry Hills. In 1930 Stace had reached a low ebb when he heard John G. Ridley preach at the Burton Steet Baptist Tabernacle: '"Eternity. Eternity." I wish I could shout or sound that word to everyone in the streets of Sydney. You've got to meet it. Where will you spend Eternity?' He later recalled that outside the church, 'Suddenly I began crying and I felt a powerful call from the Lord to write "Eternity". I had a piece of chalk in my pocket and I bent down there and wrote it. The funny thing is that before I wrote I could hardly have spelled my own name. I had no schooling and I couldn't have spelt "Eternity" for a hundred quid. But it came out smoothly in beautiful copperplate script. I couldn't understand it and I still can't.'

Until his death in 1967 Stace chalked the word 'Eternity' more than 500,000 times on the pavements of Sydney and wrote himself into Australian folklore. The word appeared in lights on Sydney Harbour Bridge on the Millennium New Year's Eve (1999–2000) and in Stadium Australia during the 2000 Olympic Games opening ceremony. In 2001 Sydney City Council trademarked the symbol to prevent its exploitation.

Brian Westlake

Brian Westlake lives. Brian Westlake leads a life of sinful sex. Brian Westlake smokes curried condoms. Brian Westlake chews up Catholics. Brian Westlake pisses on Protestants. All these reports on the doings of Brian Westlake were a common sight on Sydney's North Shore (mainly around railway stations) during the 1970s. Who was he? Who created him? A university classmate of the author claimed Brian's creator had been in his class at Sydney Grammar School. But Brian also mysteriously appeared in the Killara High School Class of '79 Reunion Book in 1999. He listed his occupation as 'spray painter'.

BUGA UP

Starting in October 1979 and really hitting their stride in the '80s, Billboard-Utilising Graffitists Against Unhealthy Promotions, or BUGA UP, were among the first 'culture jammers', attacking billboards advertising cigarettes and alcohol. Typical was their 'improvement' of a billboard advertising Peter Jackson 30s cigarettes, changing the slogan 'You're laughing' to read 'You're coughing'.

North Head Quarantine Station inmates

From 1828 to 1984 the Quarantine Station on North Head at the mouth of Sydney Harbour was the place where ships' passengers who arrived with contagious diseases were sent until they were free of illness. Many passed the time by chiselling graffiti into the rocks there, recording the names of passengers and ships, and their woes. For example:

STOP
Let weary travellers listen as we tell
The awful treatment that to us befell
On the 'Mariposa' many were our woes
'Tis a mercy we haven't turned up our toes.
Feb 1888

David Burgess and Will Saunders

In March 2003 as Australia prepared to invade Iraq, two anti-war activists painted the words 'NO WAR' in five-metre high red letters on one of the Sydney Opera House sails. They were convicted of malicious damage, sentenced to nine months' periodic detention and ordered to pay $151,000 to cover the cleaning bill.

ADVICE FOR PROFESSIONAL MEN

Pleasing manners have made the fortunes of men in all professions and in every walk of life – of lawyers, doctors, clergymen, merchants, clerks and mechanics – and instances of this are so numerous that they may be recalled by almost any person. The politician who has the advantage of a courteous, graceful and pleasing manner finds himself an easy winner in the race with rival candidates, for every voter with whom he speaks becomes instantly his friend. Civility is to a man what beauty is to a woman. It creates an instantaneous impression in his behalf, while gruffness or coarseness excites as quick a prejudice against him.

From *Australian Etiquette*, 1885

THE GREAT WAR, 1914–1918
COMPARATIVE CASUALTIES

Country	Total deaths	Total mobilised	per 1,000 mobilised	per 1,000 population
UK	723,000	6,147,000	118	16
Canada	61,000	629,000	97	8
Australia	60,000	413,000	145	12
New Zealand	16,000	129,000	124	15
South Africa	7,000	136,000	51	1
India	54,000	953,000	57	0
All allies	5,421,000	45,001,000	120	7

Source: *A Military History of Australia* (Cambridge, 1999)

SCANDALOUS SIMEON LORD

The next instance of elevation to the magistracy of a person who had been a convict, was that of S. Lord . . . [who] had been transported to the colony when young, and at first was assigned as a servant to Captain Rowley of the 102d regiment.

He afterwards lived with a female convict who had some property in Sydney, and by the profits of her trade in baking, and by his own industry, he acquired sufficient means to embark in larger speculations . . . It was at the period when his undertakings were most successful that Governor Macquarrie [sic] arrived, and found him in the possession of one of the best houses in Sydney. The circumstances of Mr Lord's life were very notorious in the colony at the time of his appointment to the magistracy, and the public animadversions that were made in the Sydney Gazette, upon several attempts, which on investigation appeared to have been made by him, to seduce two of the girls of the orphan school in Sydney, added to the general feeling of surprize [sic] with which Mr Lord's elevation to the magistracy was viewed in the colony, although these animadversions did not positively charge him with the crime. Mr Lord continued to act as magistrate at Sydney for some time, and no objection appears to have been made to an association with him by any other person than the Rev. Mr. Marsden . . .

Without stating that his elevation to that rank has had a positive influence upon his subsequent conduct, it is only justice to him to state, that his former irregularities have been latterly redeemed by the respectability of his private life . . . but his want of education, and of feelings of self-respect, have, on more than one occasion, exposed the magisterial office to contempt.

Source: J.T. Bigge, *Report of the Commissioner of Inquiry into the Colony of New South Wales*, 1822.

'THE SONG THAT MEN SHOULD SING'

The cohorts who fought when the world was young
Have their blood-red legends told,
For a hundred poets have bravely sung
The deeds of the days of old.

The story is writ of the men who fell
In desert and sun-scorched track:
The legions who served their country well –
The heroes who marched 'Out Back' . . .

But they tell us now, in their lifeless lays,
These knights of the stool and pen,
We must boast no more of the stirring days
When they fought and fell like men . . .

But the tale is best that has oft been told,
If it love of birthland bring;
And the song they sang in days of old
Is the song that I will sing . . .

We won the land from a nerveless race,
Too mean for their land to fight;
If we mean to hold it we too must face
The adage that 'might is right'.

It matters nothing what dreamers say,
When they prate that wars must cease,
For the lustful war-god holds his sway
In these piping days of peace . . .

So our lads must learn there's a sterner task
Than playing a well-pitched ball;
That the land we love may some day ask
For a team when the trumpets call.

A team that is ready to take the field
To bowling with balls of lead,
In a test match grim, where if one appealed,
The umpire might answer 'dead'!

Lt-Colonel Kenneth Mackay
The New Australian School Series Fourth Reader, Sydney, 1899.

Note: Mackay was Lieutentant Colonel in command of the NSW Imperial Bushmen's Contingent to the Boer War, and later became chief staff officer for the Australian contingents at the British Army Headquarters in South Africa. He was also the author of the novel *The Yellow Wave: A Romance of the Asiatic Invasion of Australia*, 1895.

THE MEANING OF FEDERATION

An 1890s cartoon in *The Bulletin*:

HIS TRUMP CARD
SHE (artfully): "What's the meaning of Federation, Charlie?"
HE (bashfully): "Why, Nellie (ahem), if you'll become my wife, we shall become federated." – (Nellie is pleased with the explanation).

MEAT STUDIES

Do you have a passion for meat? Are you interested in meat studies? The Cooperative Research Centre (CRC) for Cattle and Beef Quality is an unincorporated joint venture between CSIRO, NSW Agriculture, Queensland Department of Primary Industries and the University of New England.

It has three major research programs:
• Strategic science to deliver beef quality
• Innovative technologies for the beef supply chain
• Delivery of technologies to the beef business system

It also has an education and training program to create a more skilled beef industry.

ARE YOU A HOMESICK EXPAT?

Then head for one of these gatherings:

City	Event	Place	Time
Boston	The Waterhole	The Asgard, 350 Massachusetts Ave, Cambridge	First Friday of the month from 7.00 pm
Budapest	Australian Embassy Drinks Night	Champs Pub and Restaurant, D-4, VII. Dohányi utca 20	First Tuesday of the month
Chicago	Windy City Roos and Emus Aussie After Hours Club	Tavern 33, 3328 N. Lincoln Ave, Chicago (nearest EL station – Paulina)	Last Friday of the month
Copenhagen	Southern Cross Club Pub Evening	Globe Pub, Nørregade 43–45, Copenhagen (near Nørreport Station)	First Friday of the month, 6–7 pm
Dubai	Australia-New Zealand Assoc. Happy Hour	Humphrey's Bar, Dubai World Trade Centre Hotel	Second Tuesday of the month from 7.30 pm
Edmonton	Downunder Club	Wooly Bullys, 8230 103rd St	First Monday of the month from 7.30 pm
Hong Kong	Sundowners (Entry HK$50 includes light snacks and coupons for bar)	Australian Consulate General, 'Wombat Hole', 24th Floor, Harbour Centre, 25 Harbour Road, Wanchai	First Thursday of the month from 7.30 pm

City	Event	Place	Time
New York	Coffee Arvo	Ziggies, 1817 2nd Ave (cnr 94th St)	Sundays, 2.30–3.00 pm
San Francisco	Australian–American Chamber of Commerce Aussie Drinks Night	Hilton Fisherman's Wharf, 2620 Jones St (cnr Bay St)	First Thursday of the month from 6.00 pm
Seoul	Sundowners	Boomerang Bar, 11th Floor, Kyobo Building, Chongro-ku	Third Friday of the month from 6.30 pm
Singapore	ANZA Pub Night	St Gregory's Courtyard, Grand Plaza Hotel, 10 Coleman St	Last Friday of the month from 7.00 pm
Stockholm	Southern Cross Club	Dancin Dingo, Skånegatan 59, Södermalm	First Thursday of the month from 6.00 pm

FLORAL EMBLEMS OF AUSTRALIA

Australia	*Golden Wattle*
Australian Capital Territory	*Royal Bluebell*
New South Wales	*Waratah*
Northern Territory	*Sturt's Desert Rose*
Queensland	*Cooktown Orchid*
South Australia	*Sturt's Desert Pea*
Tasmania	*Blue Gum*
Victoria	*Pink Heath*
Western Australia	*Kangaroo Paw*

AUSTRALIAN TV CATCHPHRASES

Bruce – piiisss offfff!
Mrs Jackson (Noelene Brown), *The Naked Vicar Show*

Bring your money with you – bye now!
Joe Sandow, *Joe the Gadget Man*

Howdy, customers!
Bob Dyer, *BP Pick-a-Box*

Hello, possums!
Dame Edna Everage (Barry Humphries),
The Dame Edna Experience

May the good Lord smile upon you, and not let
you pass away until next time we meet.
Norman Gunston (Gary McDonald), *The Norman Gunston Show*

I love your faces!
Don Lane, *The Don Lane Show**

Do yourself a favour . . .
Ian 'Molly' Meldrum, *Countdown*

Now look at me, Kimmie, look at me, look at mueee,
look at mueee . . . now I've got one word to say to you, Kimmie . . .
Kath Day-Knight (Jane Turner), *Kath and Kim*

I'll rip yer bloody arms orf!
Aunty Jack (Grahame Bond), *The Aunty Jack Show*

Cyril said . . .
Graham Kennedy, *Blankety Blanks*

* Performed in both spoken and sign language

NSW COASTAL RIVERS

The following mnemonic will help you remember the names of all the coastal rivers of New South Wales from north to south (the Tweed, Richmond, Clarence, Macleay, Manning, Hunter, Hawkesbury and Shoalhaven):

> *Tweed Richmond Clarence Macleay*
> *was a manly hunter who*
> *shot hawks on the Shoalhaven River.*

THE *DUNERA* BOYS – AND GIRLS

The British troopship *Dunera* is best known for 'The *Dunera* Boys': more than 2000 Jewish refugees mainly from Germany, Austria and Hungary. They escaped to Britain, only to be interned as 'enemy aliens' when World War II broke out. They were transported to Australia, arriving in September 1940, along with a small number of genuine Nazis, as well as German and Italian POWs. They were interned at Hay and later at Tatura, where they did their best to re-create the Jewish culture they had left behind. After the Japanese attack on Pearl Harbor, when Australia found itself short of manpower, the internees were given the option of enlisting in the Australian Army. Many stayed on in Australia after the war.

After many years as a troopship, in 1960 the *Dunera* began a new career as an educational ship. School students would go on cruises from Britain to France, Spain, Portugal and the Mediterranean. For many, it was their first overseas trip. The cruises continued until 1967 when the *Dunera* was sold for scrap.

THREE GENERATIONS OF THE BOYD FAMILY,
AN AUSTRALIAN ARTISTIC DYNASTY

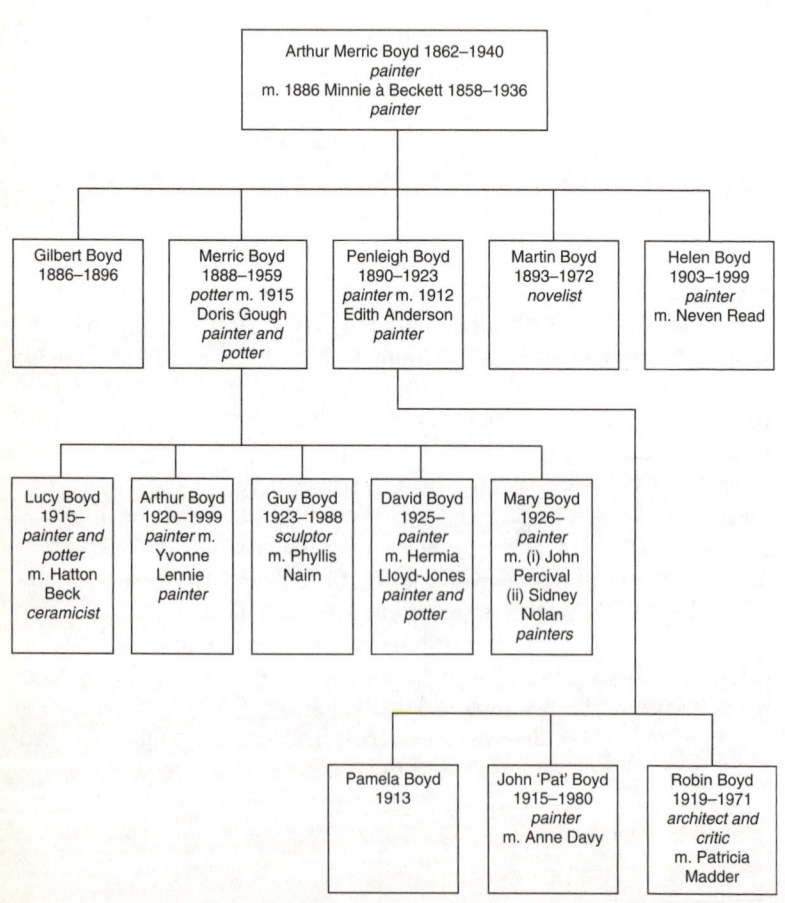

Arthur Merric Boyd 1862–1940
painter
m. 1886 Minnie à Beckett 1858–1936
painter

Gilbert Boyd
1886–1896

Merric Boyd
1888–1959
potter m. 1915
Doris Gough
*painter and
potter*

Penleigh Boyd
1890–1923
painter m. 1912
Edith Anderson
painter

Martin Boyd
1893–1972
novelist

Helen Boyd
1903–1999
painter
m. Neven Read

Lucy Boyd
1915–
*painter and
potter*
m. Hatton
Beck
ceramicist

Arthur Boyd
1920–1999
painter m.
Yvonne
Lennie
painter

Guy Boyd
1923–1988
sculptor
m. Phyllis
Nairn

David Boyd
1925–
painter
m. Hermia
Lloyd-Jones
*painter and
potter*

Mary Boyd
1926–
painter
m. (i) John
Percival
(ii) Sidney
Nolan
painters

Pamela Boyd
1913

John 'Pat' Boyd
1915–1980
painter
m. Anne Davy

Robin Boyd
1919–1971
*architect and
critic*
m. Patricia
Madder

AUSTRALIAN LIGHTHOUSES CURRENTLY IN OPERATION

Key

Height (ASL): Height above sea level

Lighthouse type:

A A 'proper' lighthouse: traditional tower with internal stair and revolving lantern.

B As above but with a fixed light such as a leading light.

G Glass Reinforced Plastic (GRP) Hut, usually solar panelled with quartz light.

L Lattice metal tower, usually with a GRP hut on top.

W In the water, i.e. a pile light or channel marker.

O Other, usually white square masonry tower.

S Lightship.

New South Wales

	Type	Height (A.S.L.)	Tower height	Position
Ballina Head/Richmond River	A	35	7	28°52′S 153°36′E
Barrenjoey Head	A	113	20	33°35′S 151°20′E
Blues Point, Cremorne	L	18	14	33°51′S 151°12′E
Bradleys Head	W	7	7	33°51′S 151°15′E
Burrewarra Point, Guerilla Bay	O	62	10	35°50′S 150°14′E
Cape Bailey, Kurnell, Sydney	A	55	9	34°02′S 151°13′E
Cape Byron	A	118	22	28°38′S 153°38′E
Clarence River, Yamba	A	41	17	28°53′S 153°36′E
Crookhaven Head	A	22	7	34°54′S 150°48′E
Crowdy Head	A	61	7	31°51′S 152°45′E
Evans Head	G	51	4	29°07′S 153°27′E
Fingal Head, Tweed Heads	A	24	7	28°12′S 153°34′E
Fort Denison (Pinchgut)	A	19	6	33°51′S 151°13′E
Green Cape	L	39	15	37°16′S 150°03′E
Grotto Point/Sydney Harbour Front	B	19	4	33°49′S 151°16′E
Henry Head, La Perouse	O	27	4	33°59′S 151°14′E
Hornby Light, South Head	A	27	9	33°50′S 151°17′E
Kiama, Blowhole Point	A	36	15	34°40′S 150°51′E
Macquarie/Sydney	A	105	26	33°51′S 151°17′E
Montague Island/Narooma	A	80	21	36°15′S 150°14′E
Nelson Head	A	39	3	32°43′S 152°10′E

	Type	Height (A.S.L.)	Tower height	Position
Nobby's Head, Newcastle	A	35	10	32°55′S 151°48′E
Norah Head	A	46	27	33°17′S 151°35′E
North Solitary Island	G	58	4	29°56′S 143°35′E
Point Perpendicular/Jervis Bay	A	95	19	35°06′S 150°48′E
Point Stephens, Fingal Bay	A	38	21	32°45′S 152°12′E
Robertson Point	W	8	8	33°51′S 151°14′E
Rosherville, or Parriwi Head	B	43	7	33°49′S 151°15′E
Shark Island	W	12	3	33°51′S 151°15′E
Smoky Cape	A	128	17	30°55′S 153°05′E
South Solitary Island	A	58	20	30°13′S 153°16′E
Sugarloaf Point	A	79	15	32°27′S 152°32′E
Tacking Point	A	34	8	31°29′S 152°56′E
Vaucluse Bay Front	B	16	8	33°51′S 151°16′E
Vaucluse Bay Rear	B	84	8	33°51′S 151°16′E
Warden Head, Ulladulla	A	34	12	35°22′S 150°30′E
Wollongong Head, Flagstaff	A	40	25	34°25′S 150°55′E

Northern Territory & Arafura Sea

	Type	Height (A.S.L.)	Tower height	Position
Bickerton Island	G	24	2	13°47′S 136°17′E
Brady Rock	G	15	2	13°40′S 136°27′S
Cape Croker	G	32	4	10°59′S 132°35′E
Cape Don/Coburg Peninsula	A	50	36	11°19′S 131°46′E
Cape Fourcroy, Bathurst Island	L	30	15	11°48′S 130°02′E
Cape Hotham	L	17	16	12°03′S 131°17′E
Cape Wessel	G	54	30	11°00′S 136°45′E
Charles Point/Port Darwin	L	39	32	12°23′S 130°38′E
Connexion Islet	G	13	11	13°50′S 136°20′E
East Vernon Island	L	12	11	12°04′S 131°06′E
Emery Point	L	18	9	12°27′S 130°49′E
Haul Round Island	G	10	7	11°54′S 134°13′E
New Year Island	L	32	30	10°54′S 133°02′E
North East Islet, near Groote Eylant	G	62	2	13°31′S 136°57′E
North West Vernon Island	G	9	9	12°03′S 131°00′E
South West Vernon Island	G	8	8	12°06′S 131°02′E
Stevens Island	G	14	6	11°32′S 136°07′E

	Type	Height (A.S.L.)	Tower height	Position
Truant Island	M	39	15	11°40′S 136°50′E
Veronica Islet	G	20	2	12°02′S 136°47′E
Warnawi Island	G	10	4	11°49′S 136°02′E

Queensland

	Type	Height (A.S.L.)	Tower height	Position
Albino (White) Rock	O	26	5	18°46′S 146°43′E
Archer Point	O	65	6	15°35′S 145°20′E
Arlington Reef	G	8	7	16°43′S 146°06′E
Bailey Islet	O	36	5	21°02′S 149°54′E
Bougainville Reef	G	15	14	15°30′S 147°07′E
Bow Reef	G	9	8	13°18′S 143°40′E
Breaksea Spit (Lightship)	S	10	10	24°21′S 153°09′E
Bribie Island, Nth end, Front	B	15	15	26°50′S 153°08′E
Bribie Island, Nth end, Rear	B	27	19	26°49′S 153°07′E
Bugatti Reef	G	9	7	20°06′S 150°17′E
Bulwer Island, Brisbane River	B	25	–	27°24′S 153°09′E
Bustard Head/Gladstone	A	102	17	24°02′S 151°46′E
Cairncross Islets	G	27	26	11°14′S 142°55′E
Caloundra Head I	A	–	9	26°48′S 153°08′E
Caloundra Head II	A	31	11	26°48′S 153°09′E
Cape Bowling Green	L	36	32	19°20′S 147°26′E
Cape Cleveland	A	64	11	19°11′S 147°01′E
Cape Moreton	A	122	23	27°02′S 153°28′E
Chapman Reef	L	18	14	12°53′S 143°35′E
Clara Group	G	65	2	22°20′S 150°43′E
Clerke Island	L	25	22	12°00′S 143°00′E
Cleveland Point, Brisbane	O	14	12	27°31′S 153°17′E
Clews Point	L	38	6	24°00′S 151°44′E
Coppersmith Rock	G	15	–	20°35′S 149°07′E
Coquet Island	G	26	22	14°32′S 144°59′E
Creal Reef	L	32	34	20°31′S 150°22′E
Decapolis Reef	G	6	5	14°51′S 145°16′E
Dent Island	A	37	10	20°22′S 148°56′E
Double Island Point	A	96	12	25°56′S 153°11′E
Duyfken Point	G	49	30	12°34′S 141°36′E

	Type	Height (A.S.L.)	Tower height	Position
East Diamond Islet	G	29	23	17°26′S 151°04′E
Eden Reef	G	6	6	14°04′S 143°55′E
Edward Island	G	109	2	20°15′S 149°10′E
Eel Reef	G	9	8	12°24′S 143°22′E
Egret Reef	G	8	7	15°28′S 145°24′E
Eshelby Island	G	56	4	20°01′S 148°37′E
Euston Reef	G	17	16	16°41′S 146°14′E
Fahey Reef	G	8	7	14°03′S 143°51′E
Fife Island	G	5	2	13°39′S 143°43′E
Flat Top Island	O	53	10	21°10′S 149°15′E
Frederick Reefs	A	33	34	20°56′S 154°24′E
Grassy Hill/Cooktown	A	162	6	15°26′S 145°15′E
Gubbins Reef	G	7	7	15°42′S 145°23′E
Hannah Island	G	24	21	13°51′S 143°42′E
Hannibal Island	G	26	22	11°35′S 142°56′E
Heath Reef	G	11	11	13°28′S 143°40′E
High Peak Island	O	70	3	21°57′S 150°42′E
Holbourne Island	G	115	2	19°43′S 148°21′E
Howick Island	G	7	6	14°29′S 144°58′E
Inset Reef	G	8	7	12°14′S 143°16′E
Island Point, Port Douglas	L	90	40	16°29′S 145°28′E
King Island	G	18	17	14°05′S 144°19′E
Lady Elliot Island	G	38	32	24°07′S 152°43′E
Lihou Reef	G	33	34	17°07′S 152°08′E
Little Bugatti Reef	L	23	24	20°01′S 150°15′E
Little Fitzroy Island	G	33	4	16°55′S 146°00′E
Low Isles	A	20	18	16°23′S 145°34′E
Magpie Reef	G	8	7	13°48′S 143°44′E
Maxwell Reef	G	9	8	14°47′S 145°18′E
Megeara Reef	G	9	8	14°28′S 144°57′E
Middle Reef	G	8	8	12°31′S 143°23′E
Miles Reef	G	6	10	14°32′S 144°55′E
Moody Reef	G	8	7	12°05′S 143°15′E
Moreton Island, Nth Point	A	25	7	27°00′S 153°00′E
North Barnard Islands	G	91	11	17°40′S 146°10′E
North Reef/Capricorn Channel	A	23	24	23°11′S 151°54′E
Palfrey Islet	O	80	5	14°41′S 145°26′E

	Type	Height (A.S.L.)	Tower height	Position
Penrith Island	O	150	4	21°01′S 149°54′E
Petherbridge Islets	G	6	3	14°44′S 145°06′E
Pickersgill Reef	G	8	7	15°51′S 145°33′E
Pine Islet	G	67	6	21°40′S 150°13′E
Pine Peak Island	O	46	3	21°31′S 150°14′E
Pinnacle Point, Hook Island	G	21	2	20°03′S 148°57′E
Piper Islands	L	12	7	12°15′S 143°14′E
Pipon Island (South)	G	26	25	14°07′S 144°30′E
Pith Reef	L	28	28	18°13′S 147°01′E
Point (Cape) Danger	O	45	20	28°10′S 153°33′E
Point Cartwright/Caloundra	A	53	32	26°41′S 153°08′E
Point Lookout	A	78	5	27°26′S 153°32′E
Restoration Rock	G	38	5	12°37′S 143°27′E
Rib Reef	G	9	9	18°28′S 146°52′E
Russell Island	L	78	17	17°13′S 146°05′E
Sandy Cape/Fraser Island	A	128	33	24°44′S 153°13′E
Saumarez Reef	G	21	18	22°39′S 153°46′E
South Barrow Islet	O	26	3	14°21′S 144°39′E
South Brook Island	L	52	18	18°09′S 146°18′E
South Head/Port Bundaberg	A	20	17	24°46′S 152°25′E
Stainer Island (Iris Reef)	L	13	11	13°58′S 143°50′E
Swains Reef, Hickson's Cay	L	10	4	22°20′S 152°43′E
Three Islands	L	27	26	15°06′S 145°25′E
Vernon Rocks	G	18	2	21°28′S 150°18′E
Waterwitch Reef	L	18	19	13°09′S 143°37′E
Watson Island	G	7	10	14°27′S 144°53′E
Wharton Reef	G	14	12	14°07′S 144°00′E
White Tip Reef	O	10	12	19°54′S 150°16′E
Wye Reef	G	7	6	12°48′S 143°36′E

South Australia

	Type	Height (A.S.L.)	Tower height	Position
Althorpe Island Rear	A	107	20	35°22′S 136°52′E
Bolingbroke Point	G	19	4	34°32′S 136°05′E
Cape Banks, Carpenter Rocks Pt.	A	25	14	37°54′S 140°23′E
Cape Bauer	G	84	2	32°43′S 134°04′E

	Type	Height (A.S.L.)	Tower height	Position
Cape Borda, Kangaroo Is.	A	155	10	35°45′S 136°36′E
Cape de Couedic/Kangaroo Is./SA	A	103	25	36°04′S 136°42′E
Cape Donington	A	33	17	34°44′S 136°00′E
Cape Jervis	A	23	18	35°36′S 138°06′E
Cape Martin, Glen Point	A	38	15	37°30′S 140°00′E
Cape Northumberland	A	45	17	38°04′S 140°40′E
Cape Spencer	A	78	9	35°18′S 136°53′E
Cape St Albans, Kangaroo Island	A	48	9	35°50′S 138°08′E
Cape Willoughby, Kangaroo Island	A	75	26	35°51′S 138°08′E
Corny Point	A	30	15	34°54′S 137°01′E
Dangerous Reef, Port Lincoln	A	11	6	34°50′S 136°15′E
Evans Island	G	17	2	32°23′S 133°29′E
Flinders Island	G	67	4	33°41′S 134°31′E
Four Hummocks, Whidbey Islands	G	120	4	34°47′S 135°02′E
Long Spit	G	9	–	34°36′S 138°05′E
Marino Rocks	A	128	15	35°03′S 138°31′E
Marion Reef	G	12	–	35°09′S 137°49′E
Middle Bank	L	11	11	33°37′S 137°33′E
North Neptune Island	G	48	4	35°14′S 136°04′E
Orontes Bank	G	11	10	34°45′S 138°00′E
Pearson Isles	G	79	2	33°57′S 134°15′E
Plank Shoal	G	12	12	33°30′S 137°28′E
Point Boston	O	12	11	34°39′S 135°56′S
Point Lowly, Whyalla	A	23	25	33°00′S 137°47′E
Point Marsden, Kangaroo Island	G	85	3	35°34′S 137°37′E
Robe, Guichen Bay	A	63	19	37°10′S 139°45′E
Shoalwater Point	O	17	15	33°40′S 137°13′E
Sibsey Island	G	26	2	34°39′S 136°11′E
Snapper Point, Kangaroo Island	L	137	7	35°45′S 138°03′E
South Middle Bank	G	11	11	33°44′S 137°30′E
South Neptune Island	A	43	5	35°20′S 136°07′E
St Francis Island	G	85	4	32°31′S 133°18′E
Tapley Shoal	G	11	11	35°02′S 137°55′E
Taylor Island	B	76	9	34°53′S 136°00′E
Tiparra Reef	O	16	–	34°04′S 137°23′E
Troubridge Hill	A	62	33	35°07′S 137°50′E
Troubridge Island	A	24	25	35°07′S 137°50′E

	Type	Height (A.S.L.)	Tower height	Position
Warbuto Point	L	36	32	34°00´S 137°33´S
Waterhouse Point	B	49	4	35°04´S 136°10´E
Wedge Island	O	206	6	35°11´S 136°29´E
West Cape, Stenhouse Bay	A	67	9	35°15´S 136°50´E
Western Shoal	G	6	6	33°11´S 137°32´E
Williams Island	G	52	6	35°02´S 135°58´E
Winceby Island	G	15	6	34°29´S 136°17´E
Yarraville Shoal	G	11	–	33°17´S 137°35´E

Tasmania

	Type	Height (A.S.L.)	Tower height	Position
Bluff Hill, Arthur River	A	52	13	41°01´S 144°37´E
Bonnet Island, Strahan	A	14	8	42°14´S 145°14´E
Cape Barren Island	G	25	4	40°26´S 148°29´E
Cape Bruny	G	93	4	43°30´S 147°09´E
Cape Rochon, Three Hummocks Island	G	40	4	40°24´S 144°57´E
Cape Sorell	A	51	37	42°13´S 145°11´E
Cape Tourville	A	126	11	42°07´S 148°21´E
Cape Wickham, King Island	A	85	48	39°36´S 143°57´E
Cat Island, Flinders Island	G	31	4	39°57´S 148°22´E
Craggy Island, Bass Strait	G	114	2	39°41´S 147°41´E
Dotterel Point, Tamar River (Front)	A	5	6	41°04´S 146°47´E
East Moncoeur Island, Bass Strait	G	102	2	39°14´S 146°32´E
Eddystone Point	A	42	35	41°00´S 148°21´E
Entrance Island, Strahan	A	10	8	42°13´S 145°13´E
Goose Island, Bass Strait	A	36	30	40°19´S 147°48´E
Highfield Point, Stanley	G	49	6	40°44´S 145°17´E
Hogan Island, Bass Strait	G	136	4	39°13´S 146°59´E
Holloway Point, Flinders Island	G	9	4	39°44´S 147°58´E
Hunter Island, Cuvier Bay	G	56	4	40°29´S 144°43´E
Ile du Nord Island	G	23	4	42°33´S 148°04´E
Iron Pot Island, Derwent River	A	20	12	43°04´S 147°25´E
Lady Barron, Flinders Island	L	48	12	40°12´S 148°14´E
Low Head, Tamar River (Rear)	A	43	19	41°03´S 146°47´E
Low Rocky Point	G	40	4	42°59´S 145°31´E

	Type	Height (A.S.L.)	Tower height	Position
Maatsuyker Island	G	140	2	43°39′S 146°16′E
Mersey Bluff, Devonport	A	37	16	41°10′S 146°21′E
North East Island, Kent Group	G	107	4	39°27′S 147°23′E
Point Home Lookout	A	57	14	42°33′S 147°57′E
Port Davey, Whalers Point	L	26	4	43°18′S 145°56′E
Rocky Cape	A	64	9	40°51′S 145°30′E
Round Hill Point	A	30	7	41°04′S 145°58′E
Sandy Cape	A	23	6	41°25′S 144°45′E
Schouten Island, Chicken Point	G	44	4	42°21′S 148°18′E
South West Island, Kent Group	G	100	2	39°31′S 147°07′E
Swan Island	A	30	27	40°44′S 148°08′E
Table Cape	A	180	25	40°57′S 145°44′E
Tamar River, Middle Channel	A	17	7	41°05′S 146°49′E
Tamar River, She Oak Point	A	11	7	41°05′S 146°48′E
Tasman Island	A	276	29	43°15′S 148°00′E
Whale Head	G	57	4	43°38′S 146°52′E

Victoria

	Type	Height (A.S.L.)	Tower height	Position
Cape Conran	L	15	5	37°49′S 148°44′E
Cape Liptrap	A	93	10	38°55′S 145°55′E
Cape Nelson, Portland	A	75	32	38°26′S 141°32′E
Cape Otway	G	73	2	38°52′S 143°31′E
Cape Schank	A	100	21	38°30′S 144°53′E
Cape Woolamai	L	112	3	38°34′S 145°21′E
Citadel Island	G	117	4	39°07′S 146°14′E
Cliffy Island	A	52	12	38°57′S 146°42′E
Coles Channel Light	W	5	5	38°14′S 144°42′E
Eastern Light, McRae	L	45	34	38°21′S 144°55′E
Gabo Island	A	55	47	37°34′S 149°55′E
Griffiths Island	A	12	11	38°24′S 142°15′E
Lady Bay Lower, Flagstaff	A	27	5	38°24′S 149°29′E
Lady Bay Upper, Flagstaff	A	33	5	38°24′S 149°29′E
Little Rame Head	G	57	2	37°41′S 149°40′E
Monash Light, Point Nepean	O	48	4	38°19′S 144°41′E
Mount Barkly	L	70	9	37°53′S 147°58′E

	Type	Height (A.S.L.)	Tower height	Position
Point Grant	L	52	19	38°31′S 145°07′E
Point Hicks	A	56	22	37°48′S 149°17′E
Point Lonsdale	A	37	21	38°18′S 144°37′E
Port Melbourne Channel, Rear	B	24	26	37°50′S 144°56′E
Port Melbourne Channel, Front	B	14	16	37°57′S 144°56′E
Portland, Whalers Bluff	A	41	12	38°20′S 141°37′E
Queenscliff, Hume	L	28	24	38°17′S 144°40′E
Queenscliff, Low	A	28	20	38°16′S 144°40′E
Queenscliff, Murray Tower	L	25	18	38°16′S 144°40′E
Queenscliff, High	A	40	25	38°16′S 144°40′E
Round Island	L	31	3	38°31′S 145°06′E
Schnapper Point	L	9	–	38°13′S 145°02′E
Split Point, Aireys Inlet	A	66	34	38°28′S 144°06′E
Wedge Light, Popes Eye Bank	W	7	5	38°16′S 144°42′E
West Channel Pile	W	11	12	38°12′S 144°45′E
Williamstown Light and Timeball	O	22	17	38°35′S 143°20′E
Wilson Promontory	A	117	19	39°08′S 146°26′E

Western Australia

	Type	Height (A.S.L.)	Tower height	Position
Adele Island	L	31	30	15°31′S 123°09′E
Babbage Island Carnarvon	L	30	18	24°53′S 113°38′E
Bathurst Point, Rottnest Island	A	30	19	31°59′S 115°33′E
Bedout Island	L	24	20	19°35′S 119°06′E
Breaksea Island, Albany	A	117	14	35°04′S 118°03′E
Browse Island	L	35	30	14°07′S 123°33′E
Buckland Hill	O	18	10	32°01′S 115°46′E
Bunbury, McKenna Point	A	14	10	33°18′S 115°39′E
Caffarelli Island, Broome	A	68	6	16°03′S 123°17′E
Cape Inscription	A	39	15	25°29′S 112°58′E
Cape Leeuwin, Augusta	A	56	39	34°23′S 115°08′E
Cape Leveque	A	43	13	16°24′S 122°56′E
Cape Naturaliste, Dunsborough	A	123	19	33°32′S 115°02′E
Carnarvon	O	27	–	24°53′S 113°40′E
Casuarina Point	A	43	15	33°19′S 115°38′E
D'Entrecasteaux Point	O	111	3	34°50′S 116°00′E

	Type	Height (A.S.L.)	Tower height	Position
Degerando Island	O	37	6	15°20′S 124°11′E
Eclipse Island	A	117	14	35°11′S 117°53′E
Escape Island	L	30	24	30°20′S 114°59′E
Foul Bay	O	92	6	34°15′S 115°02′E
Fremantle North Mole (red)	A	15	9	32°03′S 115°43′E
Fremantle South Mole (green)	A	15	9	32°03′S 115°44′E
Gantheaume Point	L	33	24	17°59′S 122°11′E
Guilderton	A	74	30	31°20′S 115°29′E
Hillarys Boat Harbour, Wanneroo	L	24	20	31°50′S 115°44′E
Imperieuse Reef, Rowley Shoals	O	30	30	17°31′S 118°57′E
Lacepede Islands, East, Broome	L	25	17	16°54′S 122°12′E
Lacrosse Island, Wyndham	O	113	3	14°44′S 128°18′E
Lesueur Island	L	20	17	13°49′S 127°16′E
Pelsaert Island	A	21	20	28°59′S 113°58′E
Point Cloates	G	39	2	22°43′S 113°41′E
Point Moore, Geraldton	A	34	35	28°47′S 114°35′E
Point Quobba	A	64	18	24°29′S 113°25′E
Red Bluff, Broome	G	48	4	17°04′S 122°19′E
Rottnest Island	A	80	38	32°01′S 115°30′E
Shoal Point	A	118	6	28°04′S 114°12′E
Steep Point, Shark Bay, Denham	G	70	4	26°09′S 113°09′E
Woodman Point	A	37	13	32°08′S 115°46′E

Torres Strait

	Type	Height (A.S.L.)	Tower height	Position
Albany Rock	O	30	6	10°43′S 142°37′E
Arden Islet	L	16	13	09°52′S 143°10′E
Bet Reef	G	8	7	10°10′S 142°49′E
Booby Island	A	37	18	10°36′S 141°54′E
Bramble Cay	L	19	17	09°08′S 143°52′E
Dalrymple Islet	G	24	23	09°37′S 143°17′E
Dove Islet	G	10	8	10°00′S 143°02′E
East Cay	G	32	31	09°24′S 144°14′E
East Strait Island	G	6	7	10°29′S 142°26′E
Eborac Island	O	39	6	10°40′S 142°32′E
Goods Island, Western Hill	G	105	5	10°34′S 142°09′E

	Type	Height (A.S.L.)	Tower height	Position
Hammond Island, Hammond Rock	G	13	2	10°31′S 142°13′E
Harvey Rocks	G	14	8	10°18′S 142°41′E
Kircaldie Reef	G	9	8	10°20′S 142°49′E
Sue Islet	G	7	5	10°12′S 142°49′E
Tuesday Islet	G	12	4	10°33′S 142°19′E
Twin Island	G	69	6	10°27′S 142°26′E
Wednesday Island	G	40	6	10°30′S 142°18′E
Wyborn Reef	L	21	21	10°49′S 142°46′E

Note: this list covers a coastline of 36,735 kilometres. The last manned lighthouse, Maatsuyker Island, Tasmania, lost its keeper in December 1995. However some still have a caretaker.
Source: Kevin Mulcahy, from *British Admiralty List of Lights and Foghorns*, Vol. K

THREE LADY BUSHRANGERS

Mary Howe ('Black Mary')
Captured (along with several other women) after a bloody raid on her tribe by the Tasmanian bushranger Michael Howe and his gang, she remained with Howe and became his lover. In 1817 the gang was ambushed by soldiers and Mary was injured and captured. According to legend, she was shot and injured by Howe himself and in revenge helped the police track him down.

Mary Ann Baker
Aged 14 Mary Ann Bugg married a shepherd, Edmund Baker. She first met Frederick Ward (later to become the bushranger Captain Thunderbolt) during the 1840s and after Baker's death claimed to have married Ward in about 1860. Mary Ann rode with Captain Thunderbolt in northern NSW and they had at least three children.

Elizabeth Jessie Hickman ('The Lady Bushranger')
Born around 1890, Jessie became a circus performer, and was a champion bareback rider and crack shot. She put her skills to use as a cattle duffer in the 1920s, hiding out in the Wollemi in NSW and evading the police numerous times. Finally in 1928 she was captured and charged with cattle stealing. Although she later returned to the bush, Jessie eventually died in Newcastle Hospital, aged 46.

SOME HIGH ACHIEVERS BY STAR SIGN

After reading Ann-Maree Moodie's *Local Heroes: a celebration of success and leadership in Australia* (Prentice Hall, Sydney, 1998) idle curiosity led me to make the following analysis of these thirty-seven randomly-chosen high achievers included in the book.

Aries
Mick Dodson
Jim Sweeney
Max Suich

Taurus
Peter Ryan

Gemini
Carl Wood
Elizabeth Jolley
Bob Joss

Cancer
Ken Done
Craig Kimberley
Daniel Petre
Neil Perry

Leo
Michael Gudinski
Sean Howard
Glenn Murcutt
Bryce Courtenay
John Laws
Frank Blount

Virgo
Gareth Evans
Baz Luhrmann

Len Evans
Vivienne James
Pru Goward
Gai Waterhouse

Libra
Ian Kiernan
Frank Lowy
Robyn Nevin
Roma Mitchell
Ian Barker
David Campese

Scorpio
Stephanie Alexander

Sagittarius
John Yu
Paul Simons

Capricorn
Adrienne Clark
Ronald Penny

Aquarius
Eva Cox

Pisces
Jeff Kennett
David Williamson

If you plot the result it looks rather like a slightly skewed bell curve with a preponderance of high achievers being born from 22 July to 22 October. You can draw you own conclusions . . .

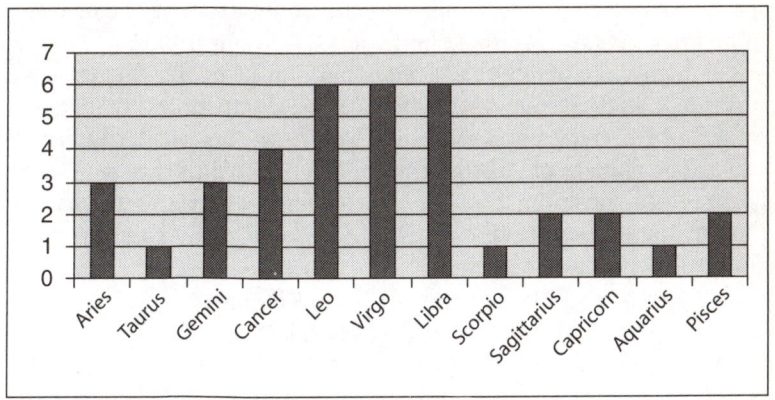

AN AUSTRALIAN UTOPIA

In July 1893, 220 men, women and children left Sydney on the *Royal Tar* bound for Paraguay – and a new life, one in which people worked together for the good of all, and men and women would be treated equally. William Lane, a journalist and political activist, was the leader of the group, and the settlement they established was called New Australia.

But Lane's utopian vision was never fully realised. Dissent soon developed amongst the group and by the end of December 1893, just two months after New Australia was officially founded, about half the population had seceded. By May the following year Lane himself had left with 62 supporters to start a new colony, Cosme. One well-known follower of Lane was the poet Mary Gilmore (then Mary Cameron) who arrived at Cosme in 1896.

By November 1902 Cosme had collapsed and its inhabitants scattered.

THE AQUATIC NATION

In no part of the world have aquatics been brought to greater perfection than in Australia. In this particular class of pastimes or sports, for it includes both, the colonies would appear to be destined to be pre-eminently foremost in the not far distant future.

It is highly creditable that a mere handful of people should have furnished, in the course of a few years, competitors against the English themselves, upon their own waters, in this peculiarly British sport. The climate of Australia has much to do with this, as also its geographical position, both of which would appear to predispose the inhabitants to betake themselves, from early youth, to the waters for sport and pastime.

Australian Etiquette, 1885

THREE AUTHORS OF AUSTRALIAN CHILDREN'S CLASSICS BORN ELSEWHERE

Ethel Turner (1872–1958)
The author of 27 novels, including the famous *Seven Little Australians*, about an all-Australian family, was born in Doncaster, England in 1872.

Ethel Pedley (1860–1898)
The author of *Dot and the Kangaroo* was born in Acton, England, in 1860. The classic Australian children's book was first published in England in 1899.

May Gibbs (1877–1969)
The author of the much-loved *Snugglepot and Cuddlepie* was born in England and arrived in Australia aged four.

INDEX BY SUBJECT

C

D

E

F

L

M

N

Q

R

S

T

U

V

W

Y

ACKNOWLEDGEMENTS

For encouragement, suggestions and answers to questions, thanks to: Bob Morgan, Scott Wickstein, Stephen Flavel, Dilum Dassanayake, Judith Hobbs, The City of Sydney History Program (Shirley Fitzgerald, Lisa Murray, Hillary Golder, Janice Cave, Margaret Betteridge, Tiina Hendrickson), Chris and Jan Macdonald, John and Shirley Stackhouse, Jennifer Stackhouse, Geoffrey Stackhouse, Johanna Cole and Kevin Mulcahy. And thanks also to my wonderful editor and the team at Random House.

ABOUT THE AUTHOR

David Morgan was born in Newcastle and grew up in Sydney. His work in the IT industry took him to Melbourne, London, Royal Leamington Spa, Chicago, Indiana, and back to Newcastle. Eventually scorning IT for his true passion, David studied history at Sydney University, gaining an MA with merit, and now works as a consulting research historian. He first found a head full of trivia rewarding some time in the late 1990s, when a weekly game of squash would be followed by the trivia quiz at the Epping Hotel, NSW, and the prizes would be free dinners at the bistro: winning most weeks, he and his teammates paid for their dinners that way. His knowledge of miscellany helped him again in 2004 when he won $250 000 on the quiz show *Who Wants to be a Millionaire*. David Morgan lives in Sydney, and enjoys being the lone male in a house full of females: his wife, daughter and two cats.